ARCANA

ALICE MASTROLEO

TAROT for
Practical People

A SIMPLE AND POP METHOD
TO LEARN CARTOMANCY

LO SCARABEO

Alice Mastroleo

TAROT FOR PRACTICAL PEOPLE
A simple and pop method to learn Cartomancy

Translation: Emily Guidoni
Proofreading: Lunaea Weatherstone
Editing: Paolo Bertazzo, Elena Delmastro
Graphics and Layout: Chiara Demagistris

©2023 - Lo Scarabeo

Facebook and Instagram: loscarabeotarot
Printed by Grafiche Stella in September 2023

Table of Contents

Foreword

"Never touch your idols: the gilding will stick to your fingers."
(Gustave Flaubert)

But we don't mind the gilding on our fingers.

That evening in Domodossola, just before the talk on Tarot cards was set to begin, Alice suddenly veered left and dashed into an '80s-themed perfume shop, the kind that can only be found tucked away in the heart of small provincial towns. It was a spontaneous move, reminiscent of a hunting dog sniffing out its prey or the sudden realization, at the last second, that you've run out of milk and decide to make a dash for the nearest closing supermarket. Intrigued, I followed her, no one else noticing our sudden disappearance, losing track of the rest of the group. Amidst all the exuberance of vibrant colors, shimmering sequins, satin, and plush decor, I felt a sense of disorientation, caught between being somewhat nostalgic for my childhood and repugned by the tacky style in fashion in those bygone years. However, Alice remained unfazed by the surrounding spectacle. She possessed an innate understanding of which fragrances were truly worthy of consideration. Together with a perfume that whispered an echo of a distant memory, she also purchased something of quite the unexpected—a peculiar Scottish headband adorned with teddy bear patterns, a fashion statement that only she knew how to pull off, where the rest of us would never stand a chance.

This serves as a testament to Alice's unrivaled sense of style and her unwavering wisdom, both of which make this book an absolute must-have. In addition to it being exceptionally practical, as promised by the title, it also offers a fun and joyful reading experience. Having shared my insights about the author, a person who knows exactly what she wants and how to navigate it, let me tell you that Alice is more than just the one who reads my Tarot cards or the person I recommend to anyone seeking guidance. Friends and acquaintances often come to me asking who they should turn to for readings or to learn the craft themselves, only to be disappointed when I reveal that I just draw Tarot cards. But why is that? Those who have even a basic acquaintance with Alice and the Arcana may have already caught on. And if you're still in the dark about what I mean, fear not, for these pages will soon illuminate your understanding.

Spoiler Alert: Alice embodies the essence of both the Empress and the High Priestess, making her an irresistible companion for engaging conversations. Her compassionate heart possesses an unwavering commitment to scrutinize and evaluate her surroundings, defying norms, and shattering stereotypes with her distinctive approach, infused with a delightful dose of irony. Having come this far, I'm sure you may be questioning why I, an artist, am writing this preface. I asked myself the same thing, and here's my answer. We both found ourselves deeply immersed in exploring the world of the Arcana. Whether they needed us or not, we certainly needed them (and by "we" I'm also referring to you, dear reader). In essence, we find ourselves immersed in the intricate handling of these sacred idols. I redraw the cards in a contemporary light, making sure I preserve their inherent symbolism, and Alice does the same, interpreting various types of decks, both ancient and modern, in her readings. After all, through the Arcana, you can develop a deep alchemical symbiotic connection—a constant flow of dormant and awakened energies. Naturally, the revelation of this shared essence with Alice felt like discovering a kindred spirit amidst the most esteemed luminaries. Filled with excitement, I eagerly invited her to read the Tarot cards I crafted, starting with the Marseille deck and later the deck inspired by Rider-Waite-Smith, during every event I hosted at my studio. Our paths frequently intertwined as we participated together in various talks, including the unforgettable one mentioned before, in Domodossola. But let's delve back into the book you hold in your hands, and why I strongly believe it deserves to be read: because within its pages, you truly capture the profound essence of the enantiodromic structure of the Tarot in all its magnificence.

The Tarot, in its wisdom, teaches us that our most grievous flaws can transform into our greatest virtues and source of strength and vice versa.

Rarely have I encountered a text that illuminates these aspects with such remarkable clarity and, above all, contemporary relevance, intertwining nuances of high and low, regal and popular.

The result is a deep acknowledgment of the full spectrum of human existence, embracing both its flawed aspects which we should be mindful of but also accept as essential to our development, and its noblest, undeniably inclusive qualities.

With an exceptional soundtrack that will accompany us throughout the pages of this book—ranging from Beyoncé to Einstürzende Neubauten—let the journey of Hero 2.0—better known as Ms. Betty—begin!

Elisa Seitzinger

Somewhere,
I must take the first step

Ever since my school days, I've always been intimidated by the thought of having to write something. Whether it's an essay, a thought, or a thesis, that dreadful blank page anxiety has always been crippling. I tend to overthink the idea and its content, and never know how to start putting it down on paper. Days would pass as I grappled with thoughts like, "Will my style be too formal?" or "Is this the right tone for this section?" However, I knew I had to begin somewhere, so I resorted to a strategy I often employ: buying time and disguising my hesitation. And here we are now, with numerous lines filling these pages, but still no real significant information written. Nevertheless, in the midst of it all, my anxiety has subsided, and I've managed to break the ice. 😇

Now, in this particular era of publishing, where countless books of questionable quality flood the market, you might wonder why another book on cartomancy, adding to the countless ones that already exist. Well, first and foremost, I was asked to write it. I've been incredibly fortunate to have crossed paths with Lo Scarabeo, a publishing house that believed I had a unique perspective to offer on a subject that has been extensively explored. But what sets it apart, you may ask? Fundamentally, the flaw in this field lies in the repetitiveness of its content. Over the years, the same ideas have been recycled time and time again, delivered in a manner that is antiquated and devoid of inspiration.

You may think this has been so due to the need to uphold a deep-rooted tradition, as the meanings in cartomancy, though not exact science as such, are generally accepted and should be maintained. However, there's more to it. Many aspects and perspectives surrounding interpretations and the use of Tarot have fallen behind, while society and individuals have progressed and evolved, resulting in an anachronistic divide between potential querents and the insights card readers have to offer. Writing a book like this is potentially a risk—a risk I have chosen to take. It's like creating a modern reinterpretation of a movie classic: it can either be a resounding success or a complete disaster, serving no purpose and only deserving of the Razzie Awards (please, Bae, don't nominate me!). In this book, I envision the opportunity to introduce you to a fresh perspective on cartomancy: one that is witty, inclusive, and never predictable. I've taken this risk because Tarot has become a significant part of my world, and I strive daily to dispel the misconceptions that tarnish its brilliance and the lingering aura of fear associated with it. I do so by explaining, clarifying, refuting, but above all, by having fun. I draw upon references from the pop culture of my upbringing because there's nothing that brings me greater joy than shedding light on why Tarot cards are our allies, how we can consciously use them, where we can discover their relevance in our daily lives, and debunking the false myths perpetuated by those with limited knowledge or insensitive practitioners in this field. Ah, it seems I've become a bit too formal now. But that's simply because I can't help but become passionate when discussing these matters!

I am filled with passion as I write this introduction, envisioning it as a spirited debate or a captivating speech that I share with you and all the souls who embrace this book, eagerly recommending and passing it on. Tarot hasn't always been a part of my life; I grew up in an environment where the esoteric was never discussed. The closest encounter with this world was through my grandmother Angela's premonitory dreams (the very same grandmother who, upon seeing a deck of Major Arcana cards on the table, warned me to put them away as they brought bad luck). No member of my family had ever engaged with the cards, except for the occasional traditional card games we play in Italy on Christmas day—until I came along.

Driven by an insatiable fascination for the enigmatic and the unknown, I embarked on my journey into the realm of Tarot in 2013. It was during that transformative year when Stella Noctis' book introduced me to a whole new world, far beyond the limited confines of the Italian Cloris Brosca's televised card readings on channel one, and the glossy leaflets that boasted of "the most exquisite Tarot decks" printed on cards of dubious quality. Since then, I have come a long way, uncovering my own distinctive approach that I now extend to you. However, let me be clear: my intent is not to spawn an army of carbon copies scattered across the globe. Quite the opposite, in fact—I hold my individuality in the highest regard and have little patience for those who merely imitate. My purpose is to craft an immersive and captivating journey for those who embark upon it, allowing these pages to resonate deeply with those who discover themselves reflected within. They have been composed with unwavering dedication and meticulous care, inviting you to explore the profound depths of Tarot with me.

You will find a piece of me within the pages of this fictional book, but my true hope is that by the end, a part of your essence shall intertwine as well. Scribble in its margins, jot down your notes, and include your favorite songs. Even color in the pages, if you so wish. What truly matters is that it serves as a guiding light on your own personal journey, just as it has guided me on mine. And remember, amidst the seriousness of studying a subject such as this, we mustn't forget to embrace a sense of fun. We should be able to laugh at ourselves and the comical and tragic events that unfold in our lives. May the wisdom of Tarot grant you the ability to observe these situations with the right perspective and insight.

Much love,
Alice Mastroleo aka Solo Redie

P.S.: This book does not favor any particular deck as its reference. We made this choice with Lo Scarabeo so that you can approach this realm with the deck that resonates most deeply with you. Moreover, it is a practical guide designed for pragmatic individuals: it does not delve into initiatory schools or purely esoteric aspects of cartomancy. Instead, its purpose is to equip you with the skills needed to read Tarot cards. This realm intertwines with mathematics, Kabbalah, religion, philosophy…the path you choose to follow is entirely up to you, and it will undoubtedly lead you in the right direction!

Ms. Betty and other characters

In this book, just like in any good piece of literature, we come across recurring characters, despite its main focus being Tarot. They make their way through these pages and, interestingly enough, also find a place in our everyday lives when we decide to put into practice the insights gained from our passionate and intense studies, whether we read cards professionally or on an occasional basis.

Let me introduce you to the central figure, who almost takes on a protagonist-like role—the driving force behind our journey, the one who instills confidence in our work as card readers while also having the power to dismantle hours of readings with a single question: "Will he/she/they COME BACK?" I'm referring to the quintessential client, whom I have named "Ms. Betty."

To truly understand her character, it's important to note that Ms. Betty defies gender norms; she can be anyone. Although she carries a feminine name, the creation of Ms. Betty was entirely serendipitous: I invented her during my teaching sessions to narrate and explain some of the most common questions participants could have received from the average querant. And so, with a burst of inspiration, Ms. Betty came to life.

While Ms. Betty doesn't have a specific gender or age, for the sake of convenience, I will refer to her using feminine pronouns.

Let's clarify something: we have all been a Ms. Betty at some point in our lives, whether during a Tarot reading or just in our everyday experiences. None of us is exempt from those timeless questions that seem to follow us relentlessly. Questions like "Will I ever find true love?" or "When will I finally tie the knot?" And in the most dramatic of moments, we may even ask, "If the Death card appears, does that mean I'm doomed?" (Yes, I've been asked all these questions over the years.)

There's no judgment toward Ms. Betty or anyone else who seeks answers. However, what I can assure you is that this little book will encourage those who open its pages to ask questions that empower them, to become the focal point of their own actions. It's about offering you, in particular, solutions and advice that go beyond relying on chance or external factors alone.

Furthermore, when it's your turn to read the Tarot or have your cards read, you'll have a clearer understanding of how to formulate your questions. This way, you can take a proactive stance toward the situations you want to unravel and clarify.

In this book, the second protagonist is no other but you, dear reader, and I warmly address you as "Bae." Whether you come from the countryside, like me, or belong to the Millennial or Gen Z generation, chances are you're familiar with the popular use of endearing terms and funky abbreviations like "Babe," "LYMI," or "Bae." As someone who embraces these delightful linguistic quirks, I feel a deep connection with all of you, regardless of your age.

That's why I love referring to my community as "Bae." Just like Ms. Betty, Bae represents individuals of any gender.

Baes are those who strive to challenge the clichés that surround cartomancy by blending tradition with the contemporary world and combining rationality with divinatory skills. They immerse themselves in the study of Tarot, seeking to learn an interpretive approach that transcends gender and age. Their goal is to provide practical insights for everyday life, ensuring clarity and leaving no room for doubt when it comes to deciphering the meaning conveyed by the cards. Moreover, they approach this powerful tool of introspection and self-analysis with a joyful spirit and a genuine eagerness to open their minds and hearts. If you resonate with this description, then you are undeniably a Bae through and through!

Then, of course, we have the Tarot cards. Divided into Major Arcana and Minor Arcana, they serve as the divinatory tool that I will be discussing in the upcoming pages. I will refer to them as "cards" or, alternatively, as "Arcana." Interestingly, in Italian, they are also known as "Lame," which translates to "Blades." This term derives from the Latin word "lamina," meaning a thin sheet of metal. It is believed that the illustrations on Tarot cards were once engraved on metal sheets before being printed. Through metonymy or a historical association with the use of metal plates, the term "lame" eventually became synonymous with the cards themselves.

Last but certainly not least, we have the readings, which provide answers to the questions posed.

The Spread of the Week (which I playfully renamed as Spreadie of the Redie a few months ago, to add a rhythmic touch to my nickname "Redie") is the spread that I diligently share on Instagram every week. It offers a glimpse into the energies that unfold during those seven days, serving as a sort of transit analysis from the perspective of Tarot.

Beginn3r

I've recently immersed myself in the captivating world of cartomancy, and it's been quite the journey. However, what surprises me is the stark contrast in people's reactions when I mention that I'm studying this art. Some respond with genuine excitement and curiosity, while others, quick to dismiss it, remind me that I have a degree and shouldn't put faith in what they consider mere superstition. It leaves me feeling torn, and at times, I contemplate giving up, wondering if I should continue pursuing this path. What's your take on this, Alice?

SoloRedie

Please don't give up! Pursuing a subject should always be about what feels right for you, no matter your educational background. Having a degree doesn't mean you can't be interested in things that differ from the scientific or rational point of view. We should follow our instincts, embrace our curiosity, and never limit ourselves when it comes to learning.

Don't let baseless comments discourage you. People often fear what they don't understand, and mastering the Tarot can definitely stir up fear in those who aren't aware of the incredible benefits it offers. But remember, their fear doesn't define your path. Never cease your pursuit of knowledge, and always bear in mind that true perfection remains elusive, even in science. At least Tarot, unlike many other disciplines, has never asserted itself as perfect or unerring!

The incredible journey of Tarot!

Let's begin by delving into the fascinating world of Tarot. The etymology of this term remains uncertain, possibly with Arabic origins, as suggested by Treccani—the most renowned Italian publishing house for its encyclopedias, dictionaries, and reference works. To ensure a comprehensive understanding, let's start by discussing the basics. Tarot is a card game comprising 78 cards. To cater to readers of all backgrounds, I will address even the most seemingly evident aspects, ensuring that everyone can follow along effortlessly.

These cards can be divided into two main groups: the Major Arcana, consisting of 22 cards, and the Minor Arcana, consisting of 56 cards. Now, let's embark on a journey to explore how Tarot cards, specifically the Major Arcana and the Minor Arcana, have made their way to us throughout history. Much like pasta or anything that has attained legendary status with its origins lost in time, Tarot cards boast diverse cultural claims and interpretations. Various claims suggest their origins trace back to Egypt, France, Italy (partial to that, naturally!), and even certain Arab countries.

The nomadic populations have undeniably played a crucial role in the captivating story of Tarot, contributing to its widespread presence throughout Europe. To avoid any further confusion within this intricate narrative, let's begin by focusing on the Minor Arcana, which bear a striking resemblance to the familiar playing cards you may have encountered while playing traditional games like Trumps or Rummy. Interestingly, evidence of a card-based game can be traced back to ancient China. This game is played with little tiles decorated with various symbols. Among these symbols, four groups of tiles representing Kings, Generals, Knights, and Pawns were prevalent. It is noteworthy that this game emerged during the early 1100s. However, the true mystery lies in how this game found its way to Europe, a mystery that remains unsolved. If I had the privilege of owning a time machine, I would embark on a journey across the lands of China, India, Persia, and finally, to the Byzantine Empire. It is widely believed that the daring adventurers of this extraordinary expedition were the Romani populations, motivated by historical circumstances and a quest for stability. As they made their way along their migratory path, not only did they bring their own customs and traditions, but they also absorbed and assimilated the diverse cultures of the countries they encountered over the centuries, thus contributing to the captivating tapestry of Tarot's origins.

A hypothesis that has intrigued historians and experts revolves around the potential spread of this game through the Crusaders. While not all the dates align perfectly, the idea is worth exploring. Picture this: we find ourselves in Asia Minor, somewhere between 1270 and 1291, where soldiers stumble upon a local card game, seeking respite between grueling battles. Upon their return to Europe after being defeated, they bring these cards with them.

However, we must also consider the influence of Arab-Islamic dominion over southern Spain, North Africa, and Sicily for six centuries. It is highly likely that during this period, a card game with four suits began to circulate, possibly inspired by the Mameluke cards. These cards, resembling the ancestors of our Piacentine cards at first glance, depict Coins, Cups, Swords, and Sticks. Decorated with aphorisms and poems, they carry numeric values ranging from 1 to 10, along with three "figures" (I use quotes here as the depiction of humans was forbidden in ancient Islamic tradition): the *malik*, the king, the *nâib malik*, the viceroy, and the *nâib thanî*, the second viceroy, having the least value.

Finally, a precise reference to the use of cards for gaming emerges from the writings of a German monk named Johannes von Rheinfelden in 1377. He states, "A game played with cards has reached us today in 1377."

We therefore have at least one solid historical testimony to rely on. Now our journey takes us to Italy, specifically to Viterbo, where the contemporary chronicler Giovanni Covelluzzo shares an intriguing account: "In the year 1379, the game of cards was brought to Viterbo from the land of the Saracens, known as Naibi." You cannot imagine the extent of my efforts to bring us here, piecing together fragments of historical clues and contradictory sources. It feels as if we are finally coming close to a full circle, as "nâib" was indeed part of the names of two figures in the Mameluke deck, and the Saracens, at that time, dominated over the entire Arabian Peninsula and extended their influence into the Middle East. It's almost like solving a murder mystery. Anyway—going back to the story—even today, "naipes" in Spanish refers to playing cards. Once the cards arrived in Italy, their popularity soared, swiftly spreading to Germany, Switzerland, France, and Belgium.

Each nation contributes its own elements of tradition, just as France did by incorporating characters from the *chanson de geste*. As we follow the Ariadne's thread that leads us to playing cards, which later evolved into the Minor Arcana, allow me to share the journey, whether true or presumed, that leads us to the Major Arcana. Regarding the origin of this segment of the deck, it is presumed that its primary purpose was educational. The Italian Naibi, with their figurative rather than numerical representation, likely played a role in the emergence of the *Trionfi*, comprising the 22 cards we now recognize as the Major Arcana. These cards encompassed 50 images, divided into five sets of ten, symbolizing

Virtues, Planets, Sciences, Muses, and Conditions of Life. Among them, familiar names start to emerge: Temperance, the Sun, the Emperor, and the Hierophant. Do they ring a bell? Excellent! We are drawing closer to familiar ground. The first deck to bear the name Tarot or Tarocchi is the renowned Mantegna Tarocchi from the early 15th century. It consisted of two series of engravings created for educational and mnemonic purposes, arranged from E to A (the rationale behind this peculiar choice remains a mystery).

Let me share some more details with you: it was eventually discovered that this deck was not actually created by Mantegna but rather it is believed to be the work of two unknown artists from his school. The shift from its original purpose as an educational and mnemonic tool to its adoption for divination happened relatively quickly, driven by people's inherent desire to seek answers and predictions using ordinary objects. Tarot decks then spread from one Italian court to another. The oldest surviving Tarot deck consisting of 22 Major Arcana is the Visconti series. When I say "series," I'm referring to three versions of this deck, each more or less complete (although none is 100% complete): the Visconti-Sforza, the Visconti di Modrone, and the Brera-Brambilla (it's hard to find a more Milanese surname than that, perhaps only Fumagalli). These Visconti decks were originally crafted for aristocrats, and their images, dating back to the mid-1400s, offer us a captivating glimpse into the customs and distinctive iconographic style of the Italian Renaissance.

The decks are beautifully decorated with intricate gold inlays, as they were commissioned by Filippo Maria Visconti and Francesco Sforza to reflect the splendid atmosphere of 15th-century Milan. As I mentioned before, the Triumphs (the name for the Major Arcana at that time) traveled from Italy across the Alps, reaching various European countries, and leaving a profound influence on the production of the world's most famous Tarot deck: the Marseilles Tarot. Around 1600, a significant revolution took place in the printing techniques used for these decks. They transitioned from being exclusively crafted for aristocratic families with gold leaf prints and limited quantities, to mass production on more affordable materials, making them readily available to a wider market.

The person who played a pivotal role in perfecting and popularizing the Marseilles Tarot, ultimately shaping their destiny and making them widely accessible, was Nicolas Conver. As a printer, publisher, and engraver at the court of France, Conver made significant contributions. It is thanks to him that we transition to the next chapter of this journey, where the Tarot of Marseille found its way into the hands of Court de Gébelin. Antoine Court de Gébelin, a prominent literary figure of 18th-century France, began with the first theory suggesting an Egyptian origin for the Tarot. More specifically, he connected the Major Arcana to certain images depicted in the Book of Thoth, the well-known book of the dead. According to Court de Gébelin (although this remains a speculative theory lacking concrete evidence), the book made its way from Egypt to Europe through the migration of Romani (Gypsy) populations, originating from regions of Asia Minor and settling in the Mediterranean basin. Coming to Court de Gébelin's aid is Etteilla, whose real name is Jean-Baptiste Alliette. Etteilla, a clever pseudonym formed by spelling his surname backwards, played a significant role in furthering Court de Gébelin's ideas.

There isn't much concrete information available about him (though I recently discovered that the rumor of him being a hairdresser is untrue). I must admit, I found the idea of him being a precursor to the famous TV personality Wanna Marchi quite intriguing. However, let me share what we do know for sure: Alliette, an occultist and esotericist, was the first to develop a prophetic method that took into account various elements. He introduced the notion that the numbers associated with each card (previously nonexistent for the Major Arcana) and their orientation when drawn played a decisive role in shaping the outcome of a card reading. These ideas further supported Court de Gébelin's belief in the Tarot's Egyptian origins. To encapsulate his ideas succinctly, Alliette created a deck bearing his stage name, intended for prophecy and occult practices.

To establish the thesis that Tarot cards are derived from Jewish culture, we must consider their association with the 22 letters of the Hebrew alphabet. This idea gained significant support from Eliphas Levi, a French occultist of the 19th century, who viewed Tarot as a key for interpreting the Kabbalah. Later, Papus (Gerard Encausse), another occultist, refined this theory by establishing a connection between the Major Arcana and the letters of the alphabet. However, it was Oswald Wirth, a Swiss scholar, writer, astrologer, and philosopher, who managed to unify these concepts and symbolize them into a single deck.

It's astonishing to think about how much people accomplished before we had televisions, when they could dedicate themselves fully to their studies. Wirth lived during the transition from the 19th to the 20th century, and his exploration of symbols as a universal language connecting various esoteric traditions greatly impacted the Tarot community. He presented a method for tapping into the collective unconscious and awakening the archetypal knowledge within each individual.

According to Wirth's theory, the Tarot deck incorporates diverse symbolic systems originating from different esoteric traditions, including Freemasonry, of which Wirth himself was a member.

Oswald Wirth's Tarot deck not only serves as a prophetic tool but also as a profound instrument for introspection and guidance during times of uncertainty. Our journey culminates in early 1900s England, where a young and talented Anglo-Jamaican illustrator named Pamela Colman Smith crosses paths with the enigmatic mystic and occultist Arthur Edward Waite. Their connection is forged through their shared membership in the esteemed Order of the Golden Dawn. Impressed by Smith's artistic abilities, Waite commissions her to create the illustrations for his groundbreaking deck. This visionary work aims to break away from traditional norms by incorporating symbolism drawn from Hermetic and Golden Dawn philosophies, while still honoring the use of archetypes in the Major Arcana.

Smith finds inspiration in the captivating drawings of the Sola Busca deck, which stands out as the first deck to depict scenes from everyday life and allegorical imagery for the Minor Arcana, departing from the repetitive suits found in standard playing cards. Smith remarkably accomplishes this monumental task in the astonishingly short span of just six months, bringing it to a completion in October of 1909. However, despite the immense success of the deck over the following century, she sadly does not receive proper compensation or recognition for her extraordinary contribution.

This exceptional creation has become the best-selling Tarot deck of all time, captivating the hearts and minds of countless individuals seeking guidance and illumination.

Pixie, the endearing nickname of Pamela Colman Smith, can be rightfully considered a pioneer among today's freelance illustrators. She embarked on a creative journey that has secured her place in history, despite receiving a paltry compensation that hardly reflected the immense effort she poured into her work.

Another intriguing Tarot deck worth exploring is the Tarot of Thoth, designed by the renowned painter Lady Frieda Harris, whose style gracefully embraces the essence of futurist art. This visionary deck, unlike the Rider-Waite-Smith Tarot, took five years to complete and boasts unique symbolic codes and individual Arcana names—unlike any of the decks I've discussed thus far.

After embarking on this fascinating journey from China to England, I am now eager to delve into the myriad ways contemporary culture has embraced the language and imagery of Tarot. It is truly remarkable to witness the profound impact these archetypal cards can have on individuals, even those who may lack the expertise to interpret them. Yet, they are incredibly fascinated, and they serve as an infinite source of creative inspiration for numerous artists.

It is truly remarkable how a timeless practice like this continues to evoke deep emotions and exert an irresistible fascination to this day. I believe this captivating power stems from its ability to be instantly recognizable—and yet shrouded in mystery.

Tarot in POP culture

From the 17th century onward, advancements in printing techniques made way for the widespread production and distribution of playing cards, propelling the Tarot to quickly traverse across Europe. It broke free from the confines of noble courts and the exclusivity of opulent, gold-adorned editions, finding its place in more affordable materials and accessible formats. The Tarot became a game of the populace, often abbreviated as "pop," and as it exchanged hands, it reached individuals who were drawn not only to its prophetic aspects but also to its allegorical and figurative nature.

Salvador Dali, renowned for using his artistic expression to challenge the boundaries of reality and infuse it with visions and paradoxes, undoubtedly felt a profound resonance with Tarot. It comes as no surprise that Dali created his own unique Tarot deck, an embodiment of the Arcana's enchantment, seamlessly blending his surreal touch. For enthusiasts of the genre, Dali's deck became a guiding companion, ushering them into a world that is both psychedelic and symbolically subversive.

Naturally, Dali, as the creator, portrays himself as the Magician, embodying the essence of limitless potential. However, he is not the only Surrealist artist who is captivated by the Arcana. Recently, a deck belonging to Leonora Carrington, a uniquely talented figure in this artistic movement, was fortuitously discovered in a private collection. In a similar vein, the painter Victor Brauner depicts himself as the Magician, aptly named "Le Surrealiste," indicating the wide appeal of this Arcanum. It is intriguing to observe the harmonious relationship between the occult and Surrealism.

While not directly associated with the movement, the artist Niki de Saint Phalle engages with vibrant colors and unconventional sculptural forms in her grand creation, the Tarot Garden. This awe-inspiring park located in Tuscany is a testament to her vision and experience. Over a span of 19 years, Niki de Saint Phalle collaborated with various multidisciplinary artists from the contemporary art world to bring each Major Arcanum to life within the garden.

Surprisingly, even the perpetually anxious Andy Warhol did not shy away from Tarot card readings. He amassed several decks and even participated in collective reading sessions in 1966. Inspired by these experiences, he made *The Velvet Underground Tarot Cards*, a short film depicting a fortune teller attempting to provide consultations to the band members amidst the chaotic revelry surrounding them.

Tarot cards have even found their way into the world of Cinema. In *Live and Let Die*, the character Solitaire, a fortune teller, makes an appearance, while Woody Allen's film *Scoop* revolves around unraveling the mystery of the Tarot Card Killer. Guillermo del Toro's *Nightmare Alley* features Toni Colette flawlessly portraying a fortune teller in an eerie and old-fashioned amusement park. Additionally, Nicolas Winding Refn, in his streaming TV series *Too Old to Die Young*, assigns each episode the name of a Major Arcanum, vividly depicting the archetypal characteristics of the protagonists in a distinct and intense manner.

Roman Polanski's film *The Ninth Gate*, which delves into the occult, showcases woodcut illustrations from the demonic book *Horrido Delomelanicon*, incorporating various Tarot images such as the Hanged Man, the Wheel, the Fool, and Death, among others.

In the recent film *House of Gucci*, we see Salma Hayek taking on the role of the unconventional Pina Auriemma, reading Tarot cards for Patrizia Reggiani, portrayed by Lady Gaga, with an interesting blend of Italian and American accents.

The fashion world, too, has been captivated by the fascinating Tarot. Dolce & Gabbana's fragrance collection in the early 2000s drew inspiration from specific Major Arcana, while Maria Grazia Chiuri's remarkable Autumn-Winter 2021 collection for Dior was influenced by Matteo Garrone's short film. The collection takes us on a visual initiatory journey through the 22 Arcana, with each look carefully crafted based on the stylistic study of the Visconti-Sforza deck.

Even Gucci has embarked on this journey with its "Ouverture of Something That Never Ended" collection, where each ensemble was envisioned and illustrated as a representation of a Major Arcanum. It becomes evident that every form of art has embraced this captivating and evocative realm. As we move forward, it is highly likely that more companies, communication agencies, and luxury brands will draw inspiration from the Tarot for their products or marketing strategies. However, there is a risk of misusing and distorting its essence solely for commercial purposes—a phenomenon one might call "Tarot-washing." In contrast, my mission is to make this medium accessible, blending it with pop culture while honoring its mystical and esoteric roots. I strive to breathe new life into tradition while preserving its inherent respectfulness and reverence.

"Never cross your legs" and other false myths seen through the lens of a pragmatic individual

It was a family Easter lunch from a few years ago when I thought of bringing a small deck of Major Arcana cards to engage in some lighthearted practice with my relatives. It seemed like a great opportunity to have a bit of fun and playfully introduce them to the world of Tarot, without getting too deep or serious about it. Little did I know the reaction it would elicit. You see, my family had never been exposed to anything belonging to the esoteric or shown any interest in Tarot readings. I, too, didn't consider myself as one of those gifted individuals who possess "the sight." But, regardless, I was excited to share this mystical realm with them. As I brought out the deck, the atmosphere shifted. I could feel a sense of unease emanating from my grandmother. Her voice trembled as she shouted, "No! You shouldn't use Tarot cards! They bring bad luck!" It was clear that the mere sight of the cards stirred something deep within her. In that instant, I realized the power of superstition and the diverse perspectives people hold regarding the Tarot. Despite my intention to bring some joy and curiosity to the gathering, I couldn't ignore the underlying unease and the cautionary tales ingrained in my family's collective consciousness. It served as a reminder that the Tarot holds different meanings for each individual, shaped by their own experiences and beliefs.

You can imagine how my face turned to stone in a split second. Now, brace yourself for an intriguing revelation: my grandmother, much like the other women on my mother's side of the family, isn't what you'd call a devout believer, nor does she hold any particular affection for the clergy. So, her reaction to Tarot turned out to be entirely unexpected. It wasn't driven by any Catholic fervor, but rather an underlying fear of the cards. When I inquired about the reason behind this apparent aversion, she struggled to provide a concrete answer. To this day, I remain in the dark as to why my grandmother views Tarot as a bearer of trouble. In the meantime, my grandmother has come to accept my decision to pursue this path, and she doesn't get upset when I call her right before a reading and then have to abruptly end the conversation. She simply tells me, "as long as you're happy" and we both find comfort in that. So, is it really true that Tarot cards bring bad luck? I've looked through studies from MIT and the Polytechnic Institute, hoping to find concrete evidence linking unfortunate events in human life to the use of Tarot cards, but I came up empty-handed.

Jokes aside, let's consider the fact that human beings often have a tendency to blame others for their misfortunes or failures. This inclination to shirk responsibility has led some individuals to be labeled as wicked or bearers of misfortune, resulting in historical instances of witch burnings and subsequent isolation (fortunately, we've moved past those dark times). Take, for instance, the harm done to Mia Martini—a very famous Italian singer, songwriter, and musician during the 1970s—all because someone in the entertainment industry started spreading the baseless rumor that she brought bad luck. This serves as a poignant reminder of how misguided it is to attribute the power of causing misfortune to a person or object, rather than accepting that sometimes things simply go wrong on their own, and we cannot exert direct control over everything. When it comes to Tarot cards, there is absolutely no scientific evidence that suggests reading them, having them read to you, or simply being involved with them can bring about bad luck. Period. Instead, let's try to understand what it is that triggers our fear of this prophetic tool. Does the idea of a stranger being able to delve into intimate aspects of your life unsettle you? That's completely understandable. However, it's important to remember that Tarot functions as a mirror, revealing hidden aspects of yourself and shedding light on them. Embracing and working with these darker elements is key, so there's no need to fear them.

Are you anxious that a fortune teller might disclose things you'd rather not know? I assure you that if you already practice the valuable habit of self-analysis, their revelations won't come as a surprise to you in the least. If the thought still sends shivers down your spine, it indicates that you may not fully know yourself, and what is being offered to you is an invaluable opportunity to gain insight and deeper self-awareness. Do the cards bearing the names Death or Devil strike intense fear within you? It's crucial to remember that behind these labels, used to identify the Major Arcana, lie archetypes and meanings that differ from what you might imagine. By delving into the world of Tarot through study or seeking guidance from an expert, you can uncover the legends and myths surrounding Tarot readings. One myth that has always intrigued me is the association of Tarot with the devil. As I mentioned earlier, I want to firmly dispel this misconception. Evil resides within individuals, not within the tools they use! Here's an interesting fact related to a movie you might be familiar with, *The Ninth Gate* (a must-watch for Johnny Depp fans). The woodcut engravings featured in *The Horrid Delomelanicon*—a book believed to be written by Lucifer himself—actually contain images taken from the Rider-Waite-Smith deck! However, this is the only link in the film—and completely fictional—between Satan and the Tarot. Now that we've addressed this crucial point, let's debunk some other common myths that you've probably come across. Should you cross your legs? It was a question that consumed my thoughts during the early days of my Tarot practice. I would politely ask anyone sitting across from me, even during online readings, to avoid crossing any part of their body. I believed that crossing limbs could disrupt the natural flow of energy. Ironically, I found myself being the main culprit, often unable to resist the urge to twist and entwine my own legs. However, as I progressed in my practice, I came to realize that the true essence of energy transmission lies in presence and intention. It's about creating a space of open receptivity and attentive listening from both sides. So, fear not! Whether legs are crossed or not, the energy continues to weave its way, and offering guidance to those seeking it. When it comes to online consultations, which happen to be my preferred method, they truly work wonders! The beauty of it is that the true connection goes beyond physical presence. In many instances, conducting sessions with individuals on the other side of the screen in the comfort of their own homes has proven to be immensely beneficial. It fosters a sense of relaxation and confidence, enabling them to open up more freely during our interaction. However, have you ever considered those who give card readings mere quacks? If you haven't, kudos to you! But if you have, I can understand how such an idea may have been shaped by the years of questionable characters appearing on private television broadcasts. Some of them got people to phone them on super premium rate telephone numbers, leaving you with an exorbitant phone bill. And let's not forget the money scammers talking you into buying various baubles to supposedly enhance the power of their predictions. Italy has its fair share of such characters, and one example is Maestro Do Nascimiento, also known as Màrio Pacheco, the infamous right-hand man of Italian telesales TV hosts Wanna Marchi and Stefania Nobile during the latter stages of their television career. Notorious for their fraudulent cartomancy practices, lottery number announcements, and repeatedly scamming their customers, employing manipulative tactics to coerce them into making continuous purchases under the threat of being cursed. I have received numerous testimonials from individuals in this sector who have shared their experiences of being associated with television scams like Wanna Marchi simply because they have mentioned reading Tarot cards to their friends or family. Unfortunately, even to this day, there is a tendency to generalize and link Tarot with fraudulent activities. However, as I said earlier, it is the intention behind the practice that determines its integrity, and by operating in an honest and transparent manner, we can gradually restore credibility to this field. Another misconception is the belief that reading Tarot cards requires a special gift or that knowledge must be passed down. While it is true that some families may have a tradition of Tarot reading, it is not a universal rule that everyone within the family shares the same inclination or passion. Talent or skill should not be limited to something that is solely passed down through bloodline. Cartomancy is a fascinating field that requires dedication, discipline, and a willingness to learn. While having a natural sensitivity or a genuine interest in esoteric subjects can be an advantage, it's important to remember that individual drive can be more powerful than family influence. Now, you may have heard the belief that individuals born under water signs (such as Cancer, Scorpio, and Pisces) have a greater inclination toward the occult and uncovering hidden truths. While there may be some truth to this notion, it's crucial to recognize that personal inclinations can vary greatly. I have encountered individuals with prominent earth signs in their birth charts who display a profound interest in divination, just as I have come across individuals under water signs who show little fascination for these practices. Astrological values can provide some insight, but they don't dictate one's affinity for the esoteric or their aptitude for cartomancy. Ultimately, it's the individual's passion that determines their path. It seems that a combination of factors, including astrological influences, cultural background, and personal curiosity, contribute to one's fascination with these realms. Therefore, even if your Sun doesn't reside in Pisces or Jupiter in Scorpio, but you harbor a genuine passion for cartomancy, rest assured that you're on the right path!

Lastly, let's dispel the misconception that Tarot cards hold sway over our lives. A Tarot reading provides potential solutions and advice, but it's always our choice whether to embrace or disregard them. The power to enhance our circumstances ultimately lies within our own hands.

If I sense that a situation might take a negative turn, I don't dwell on it. Instead, I take action to steer it toward a more positive outcome. The purpose of my readings is to inspire and uplift the consultants, rather than bring them down. The key lies in our willingness to participate and our ability to find strength in the guidance provided by the person interpreting the cards. I truly hope I've helped you gain more insight and a better understanding of this fascinating realm. Let's now move on to the next chapter!

How to choose your own deck (If you haven't been given one as a gift)

If you've purchased this book, chances are you've decided to embark on a fascinating journey into the immense world of cartomancy. Filled with enthusiasm and good intentions, you may encounter an obstacle along the way: the misleading myth that your first Tarot deck, or subsequent ones, must be received as a gift or, even better, handed down through generations. Imagine these Tarot decks, worn and weathered from years of use, passing from one person to another. While this idea may hold a certain charm, it's time to unveil the truth about this legend—and I must say, it's nothing short of absurd! Had I waited for someone to give me a Tarot deck as a gift, I'd still be standing idle, perhaps jotting it down on my Christmas wish list year after year or resorting to desperate measures like begging random strangers outside bookstores, to hoping for some generous soul to pass down theirs. Thankfully, the beauty of personally choosing a Tarot deck lies in the ability to examine it closely, delve into its unique characteristics, explore its colors and illustrations, and ultimately, find the one that resonates with us best. This process allows us to create a personal connection with our deck, ensuring it becomes a true reflection of our individuality. If you're just starting out, my advice is to begin with a classic deck that has a timeless and straightforward symbolic structure, rooted in tradition. Some examples of such decks include the Marseille Tarot, the Rider-Waite-Smith Tarot (known for its vibrant and expressive illustrations that make it easy to interpret using your own intuition), and the Wirth deck, which is also based on the Marseille tradition and features clean, well-defined artwork with beautiful, lively colors. There are also contemporary variations on the classic Tarot theme that offer a fresh and modern take on the original versions. For instance, the *Vintage Tarot* and the *Black and Gold Edition* are artistic reimaginations of the Rider-Waite-Smith deck, both expertly crafted by Lo Scarabeo. These alternative decks bring a contemporary touch while still maintaining the essence of the traditional Tarot. If you already have a Tarot deck, you're in for a wealth of options. In my opinion, practicing card reading, like any other pursuit, shouldn't be a financial burden. There's no need to go break the bank buying loads of Tarot decks when you often end up favoring just one anyway! Resist the temptation to splash out every time a new deck hits the market. Instead, carefully consider whether a particular deck resonates with you, if the illustrator's style aligns with your personal taste and emotions, and ultimately, if it truly speaks to you. Keep in mind that you can often find secondhand decks online or at flea markets. In which case, do check that all 78 cards (or 22 if it's a Major Arcana-only deck) are present and in good condition—you don't want the cards to tear when handling them. Once you have a deck, don't forget to cleanse it before use, then you will be ready to embark on your Tarot journey. What factors come into play when choosing one Tarot deck over another? Certainly, the appeal of the illustrations and colors is paramount. Personally, I find the Marseilles Tarot a bit lacking in depth, somewhat two-dimensional and flat (I hope I won't make too many enemies here, forgive me, Tarot enthusiasts!). The stark white background fails to evoke the emotions I desire. Thus, opting for a design that truly resonates with you can be key in motivating you to use that particular deck. Another aspect to consider is inclusivity. If you aim to reach a wide range of individuals with your readings, selecting a deck that features non-anthropomorphic figures or a representation that goes beyond traditional archetypes can help ensure that anyone receiving the reading can see themselves reflected. In recent years, several decks with a queer focus have emerged, aiming to bridge the interpretive gap tied to traditional depictions, where the Empress is typically represented as a woman and the Emperor as a man. These decks seek to provide a more inclusive and diverse perspective, expanding the possibilities of interpretation beyond binary concepts. By considering these prerogatives, you can find a deck that not only visually resonates with you but also aligns with your values and the kind of readings you wish to offer. Another factor to consider is your personal interests and passions. Are you a fan of a particular illustrator, TV show, or movie series featuring vampires, witches, or fantasy creatures? There are Tarot decks available for each of these interests; you just need to do a little searching to find a deck created by someone who shares your love and has crafted cards that perfectly resonate with your inclinations. Here's a piece of advice: start slowly with your deck selection and try to use the same cards consistently after purchasing them. This way, you can build an intimate bond based on trust and familiarity. It's important not to buy cards merely to satisfy the urge to own the latest deck, only to feel no real connection to any of them. I can assure you that even though I have many decks, I often find myself gravitating toward the same two or three with which I have a special relationship formed through a true emotional connection. By taking your time and allowing yourself to develop a deep connection with your chosen deck, you'll enhance your Tarot readings and cultivate a meaningful bond with the cards.

How to prep a new deck for readings

After finally selecting the deck to kickstart your practice, you enthusiastically tear away at the wrapping, excited to flip through the silky-smooth cards, unleashing that unique and distinctive "straight out of the packaging" fragrance. They're like a precious treasure in your hands. Yet, a dilemma arises. Should you purify them? Should they be consecrated or baptized in some way? You turn to the internet, stumbling upon rituals that may not necessarily resonate with you. Perhaps you're already familiar with magical practices, but as the title of this book suggests, you're a pragmatic individual who isn't keen on blending the magical aspect with Tarot prophecy. Don't worry, Bae, I got you. Now, let me explain what cleansing entails and how you can make the deck truly your own, without relying on spells or magic formulas.

When purchasing items that we intend to use regularly, such as a pan or a dress, we instinctively tend to want to wash them before using them. This precautionary step is taken because we are unaware of their origins, the processes they underwent before landing on the shelves, and the numerous hands that have come into contact with them. Despite knowing that this is not the case, there's a natural desire to want things to be truly ours, and the only way to accomplish this is by giving them a thorough wash with soap and water. So, why not apply the same principle to your new Tarot deck?

Although we can't compare the deck to a pan, it is still a personal item that has passed through the hands of many and accumulated different energies that are foreign to us. How can we purify it? Certainly not with soap and water in this case, but with tools that are readily available in our homes or easily obtainable at low cost.

The first thing you'll need is coarse salt, a timeless remedy known for its ability to neutralize energies, especially negative ones. It's a simple yet powerful cleansing tool. Just take a pouch about the size of a deck of cards, place your cards inside it, and add a handful of salt. By the next morning, your cards will be revitalized, fresh and ready to use.

Next, we have smoke. You can use incense in any form you have available, whether it's crystals, cones, or sticks, or even a smudge stick. When you light it up, it becomes the perfect tool to cleanse your cards. You can pass each card through the smoke individually or treat the entire deck as a whole. As you watch the delicate wisps of smoke, take a moment to relax and feel the connection forming between you and your newly purified deck.

Modern_luna

Hey Alice! I've got a question: Is palo santo considered a smudge? I'm a bit confused about the difference between incense and palo santo. Mind shedding some light on it? Have a great day!

SoloRedie

Let me explain what a smudge is in a nutshell. It's basically a bundle of herbs tied together with a string which is burned for cleansing and purification. There are premade smudges available, with white sage being the most well known. However, it's important to be mindful when using ingredients like white sage or palo santo, as they don't originate from our Italian or European culture. We don't want to use the traditions of other cultures without truly understanding their meaning and significance.

So, what's the solution? Luckily, the Mediterranean region offers a wide array of herbs that are easily accessible, such as rosemary, lavender, olive, and common sage. Choosing or even crafting your own smudge using these local herbs is the ideal way to go! All you need to do is gather your favorite herbs, tightly tie them together with kitchen twine, and let them dry. After a few weeks, they'll be ready to be burned, and you'll have the satisfaction of making this moment very personal.

Now, about palo santo. It's a type of wood that contains resin and is typically found in stick form. When burned, it releases its aroma through the resin. However, it's important to note that palo santo belongs to the South American shamanic tradition, and its cultivation can sometimes raise ethical concerns. Therefore, it's perfectly fine to opt for alternative solutions that have a low environmental impact and are culturally closer to you.

To keep your deck cleansed, you can place it back in its original box or choose a suitable fabric bag. There are many options available for purchase, but if—like me—you're into recycling and saving you can also create your own bag or just find a fabric bag that fits the deck and consider adding some coarse salt for extra purification. When you're done with a reading, there's no need to arrange the cards in numerical order. Simply turn them all to their upright side to "reset" their energies. To get acquainted with a new deck, carry it with you during the first few days, take your time to study the artwork, and contemplate each card individually—trying to understand what it reminds you of or what thoughts it triggers.

A friendly reminder: when conducting your readings, it's advisable to use a dedicated tablecloth or scarf exclusively for this purpose. I'm not here to lecture, but it's important to create a distinct space for your readings. Avoid using the same tablecloth that you've used for eating or other activities. By using separate elements for your practice, you help establish a sense of intimacy and exclusivity that enhances the experience.

How do Tarot cards really work? The (nonexistent) mystery unveiled

Now is the perfect time to tell you the story—feeling a bit like Papa Beaver right now, and I even look like him with my prominent teeth—of how often I find myself discussing Tarot with people I've just met. Their reactions vary from disdain to pity when they tell me with a somewhat perplexed look on their faces: "But I don't believe in Tarot." Although I do not take this personally as I am not the creator of Tarot, I find it more intriguing than offensive. Usually, behind such statements lies a profound lack of knowledge of the Tarot realm and its true purpose, or at the very least, a misconception around what a Tarot reading truly entails.

Let's begin with the premise that we can hold beliefs in various things, such as religion, or different gods and goddesses, or even personal values. For instance, I might believe in the God of Lasagna, even if it may elicit a skeptical reaction. It is worth noting that believing in yourself can be profoundly constructive and seeking guidance through card consultations can aid introspection. However, believing in the efficacy of Tarot readings may be met with skepticism. This skepticism undermines the inherent value of introspection, as it suggests that what lies within us is not authentic, thereby invalidating our emotions, untapped potential, and the guidance that Tarot can offer to illuminate our path and facilitate personal growth. But how does Tarot actually function? I shall attempt to provide a concise explanation, avoiding unnecessary tangents. Firstly, let me share a piece of news that may disappoint you: Tarot cards do not predict the future, or at least not with absolute certainty. I can almost hear the faint murmurs of disappointment in the background. Indeed, it is unlikely that the cards can provide a definitive answer to questions like, "Will I become immensely wealthy?" or "Will I find the love of my life?" unless these events are expected to occur within a few months from the time of inquiry.

Using Tarot cards as a means to evade responsibility by seeking answers to questions without making any effort or taking direct action leads to a lack of personal accountability. This approach hinders introspection and makes you less likely to put yourself out there and push your boundaries through trial and error and embracing risks. The true efficacy of Tarot cards emerges when we recognize discontent in our lives and actively desire to bring change. It is at this point that knowing ourselves better becomes crucial—an understanding of our strengths as well as an awareness of the weaknesses that may hinder our progress. This self-awareness enables us to effectively work on those weaknesses, empowering us to take proactive steps toward resolution and personal growth.

By navigating the present with wisdom, while taking our past into careful consideration, we have the power to shape our future. This is how the future truly comes to light during a reading, as we perceive it as a potential outcome of our actions. Let me provide an example. If I pose the question, "How will this situation unfold, and what can I do to avoid any mishaps?" and shortly after a card appears reversed, in it lies the advice on how to avoid any unfavorable outcomes. However, it is ultimately our choice whether to take that advice or not. This is the only way the future is considered in a reading—by examining the consequences of my present actions. It is not card reading, but rather clairvoyance, that can offer insights into our future trajectory. Of course, there are individuals gifted with the ability to predict the future, and they may incorporate it into their practice, but not all card readers are clairvoyants.

How is it possible for the cards to accurately depict the querent's current situation? It's challenging to provide a purely rational explanation, even for someone like me who tends to be pragmatic. However, it's important to remember that not everything in life can be explained solely by numbers and formulas. After careful consideration, I've come to the realization that a reading is an exchange of energy, where information flows between the reader and the seeker. It is through this energy that the cards are drawn and arranged in a specific sequence, which is always accurate because it truly mirrors the inner state of the querent at that precise moment.

If you learn to use empathy without getting carried away with personal interpretations, the Tarot's language can help you understand the situation you're facing. It allows you to see things from the perspective of the person seeking guidance and translate the card images into their emotions. You don't need any tricks or magic to make the Tarot work. Everything you need is already within you; you just need to activate it. So, keep going and get ready to make things happen, dear Bae.

Insights on the age and gender of Tarot cards

When I first approached the Minor Arcana cards, I encountered a much more significant obstacle compared to the Major Arcana. Not only were the Court cards strictly divided into binary gender (similar to the anthropomorphic Major Arcana), but it was the interpretations associated with them that left me feeling disheartened. It became evident that the authors had simply regurgitated information without any critical thinking, merely passing on what they had learned or read from others. The meanings assigned to the Kings, Queens, Knights, and Pages were rigidly categorized into men and women, except for the Page, which held some degree of uncertainty as it could be interpreted as either male or female depending on the card system. Breaking free from this restrictive framework felt almost impossible, and it seemed irreverent to question it, as Tarot cards were believed to always convey the truth. Are we really so certain? Especially when we assign such rigid meanings to each card? And what about the exceptions, which have always existed but are gradually finding their place in the world, thanks to the hard work of activists and passionate individuals? Where do they fit in? How can we expect Tarot cards to serve as a true guide if they don't allow for personal identification, where people feel seen, heard, and represented? Allow me to share something with you—let's start looking at the cards as images and archetypes, rather than strict representations of reality. How many times, after a long day at work, have I come home to find my boyfriend with dinner ready and the laundry done, and thought of him as embodying the Empress? Or that time when I took the initiative to share my love for Tarot on Instagram, feeling like a true Magician? If we stick to rigid gender interpretations in the Major Arcana, we create a barrier that prevents our readings from aligning with the person in front of us. Insisting on finding an old woman in a specific situation just because the High Priestess card appears is limiting. Let's break free from these constraints and think outside the box! Traditional Tarot decks were crafted during a time when nonbinary individuals, people of diverse ethnicities, and those with disabilities were far from being the norm. However, even then, the characters depicted in these decks held symbolic, archetypal meanings rather than literal representations. When using such decks for readings, it is crucial to look beyond the imagery and embrace a more inclusive approach. We mustn't assume someone's gender identity based solely on their physical appearance. Instead, a helpful tip would be to kindly ask for their preferred pronouns before we begin the reading. Likewise, when exploring matters of love, it's important not to hastily jump to conclusions about someone's sexuality. For instance, if the Emperor card appears, it doesn't automatically imply that the person's partner is male.

By acknowledging the historical context of traditional Tarot decks and adopting a progressive mindset, we can go beyond what meets the eye and create readings that are respectful and inclusive. If you prefer a Tarot deck that doesn't rely on specific gender connotations, there are several options available that reinterpret the classic imagery. For instance, the *Tarot of Pagan Cats* by Magdelina Messina and Lola Airaghi offers a fresh perspective by incorporating feline motifs into traditional Tarot symbols. Another alternative is the *Tarot of the Gnomes* by Piero Alligo and Antonio Lupatelli, published by Lo Scarabeo, which presents a whimsical and fantastical take on the Tarot archetypes. Additionally, the *Crow Tarot* by MJ Cullinane provides a unique interpretation through its captivating artwork. This wider range of imagery makes it easier to steer clear of expected associations and explore a more inclusive interpretation of the cards. Another aspect to consider is the age of the characters depicted on the cards. The Magician, the High Priestess, the Hierophant, the Hermit, and the Fool are archetypal figures that are often portrayed as either very young or significantly mature. It's important to clarify that when I mention "mature," I am referring to their wisdom and life experience, rather than simply being old. Although visually they may appear as older individuals, the interpretation goes beyond just age. During the initial stages of my studies, I encountered a prevailing notion that the High Priestess card represented an older woman. This association presented a dual constraint, linking both gender and age. However, as I delved deeper into practice and conducted readings, I encountered numerous instances where young women strongly resonated with the Hierophant card. They exhibited qualities of responsibility, carrying the burdens of their families and demonstrating a level of maturity well beyond their years. Similarly, I came across older gentlemen who related to the Magician card, symbolizing a phase in life where they found themselves in repetitive patterns. Therefore, it is essential to keep in mind that the age depicted in the Tarot cards signifies the stage we have reached in a our life journey. This applies not only to the anthropomorphic figures of the Major Arcana but also to the Court figures of the Minor Arcana. With a clear understanding of this concept, we can now embark on our journey through the 22 Major Arcana without being misled by their appearance!

The secret of
the Reversed Card

There comes a point in every Tarot reader's journey when you encounter people and fellow professionals in the field who ask if you read cards reversed.

No need to break out in a cold sweat—there isn't a definite right or wrong answer to this question. The truth is, there are simply different methods, and each one deserves recognition. Admittedly, reading the cards upright or reversed, or even solely upright, can bring about slight variations in meaning during a reading.

However, the core message intended to be conveyed often remains the same.

Personally, I have a preference for reading the cards reversed, and there are two key reasons for this. Firstly, I want the person sitting in front of me to visually understand that there's a block or an unexplored opportunity in their situation, and I want them to be consciously aware of it. In other words, I like to open their eyes and help them find the motivation and drive to make the most of their circumstances. Secondly, I find it more effective to have a clear distinction between the meanings of the Arcana based on the direction in which the cards appear, rather than integrating them all solely in the upright position.

The common misconception about reversed cards is that they represent the negative counterpart of their upright version, carrying notions of tragedy and apocalypse as if they were works by Euripides (the one who wrote Medea, and that says it all). Let me assure you, Bae, that nothing could be further from the truth. And as you know, I am a big fan of the truth, so let me explain in detail the true meaning of the reversed cards, how to interpret them with a grounded perspective (except for the Hanged Man, who is actually reversed when his feet are on the ground), and how to harness their energy to the fullest.

To become better acquainted with reversed cards, it's crucial to cultivate a mindset that sees them as opportunities that emerge from challenging circumstances. Instead of perceiving a stumble or a difficult moment as a setback, we can view it as a chance to rise again, start afresh, or even enhance ourselves. This perspective is instrumental in our personal growth, as it prevents us from dwelling solely on misfortune and getting absorbed in pain (although acknowledging our pain can be beneficial, it shouldn't consume us entirely).

Consider this: When we stumble and scrape our knees, do we stay on the ground, nursing our wounds like Peter Griffin in that well-known scene, endlessly bemoaning our suffering? Or do we pick up our strength, put a band-aid on the wound, and try to be more careful next time? The purpose of highlighting the negative aspect of a card is precisely to provoke a response, inspiring us to take action!

Reversed cards can unveil an additional layer: the hidden potential we possess to navigate through specific situations. We should make use of the resources at our disposal, typically kept for emergencies, to effectively change the dynamics in our favor. The hidden potential of a card may remain unseen when the card is unfavorable, but we can shed light on it like the lantern of the Hermit. Empowering Ms. Betty to unleash her untapped potential becomes our most impactful action, for which she will undoubtedly be grateful, as—with our support and that of the cards—she learns to truly harness it.

Consider, for instance, the scenario in which the Emperor card emerges reversed during a reading. How does Ms. Betty perceive her personal power? How skillfully can she assert herself and make her voice heard? To what extent do external influences impact her ability to take initiative? By encouraging her to express herself, make independent decisions, and resist waiting for others to decide for her, we activate her inner resources—that hidden potential I mentioned earlier—thereby unlocking the true essence of this Arcanum.

Another aspect that shouldn't be overlooked is that certain reversed cards don't necessarily carry a negative connotation. Instead, they indicate a defensive mechanism employed by the person being consulted to respond effectively to a distressing trigger that puts them under pressure. It is crucial in such cases to understand the context in which the reversed card appears and engage in a conversation with the individual to comprehend why they feel the need to shield themselves.

For instance, consider the Empress card, where emotional detachment could result from becoming overly invested in a situation or a person who hasn't reciprocated their emotional investment. It's as if Ms. Betty had built a dam to contain her emotions as much as possible. Although this instinctive reaction may offer temporary relief, our role is to gently encourage her to gradually allow her emotions to flow again, preventing a state of stagnation.

A small note: I don't use reversed cards with the Minor Arcana. To determine whether unconstructive interpretations are arising, I pay attention to two elements: the presence of multiple Swords or an overall imbalance where one suit prevails instead of a balanced mix of all four suits.

Let's recap: Reversed cards act as warnings, indicating energy disruptions or obstacles that need to be addressed. They provide us with opportunities to restore balance and overcome stagnation. Our goal is to explore the upright meanings of the cards and work toward understanding their intended interpretations.

THE MAGICIAN

I · A smiling swindler · THE MAGICIAN

The Magician embodies this description perfectly: he's sly, charming, a bit of a flirt, and will deceive you with a smile, but he also possesses great eloquence and enthusiasm. Unfortunately, this card is often overlooked—I therefore hope to shed light on its true value and give it the justice it so deserves—especially since it's the first card in the deck! Our journey into the Wheel of Tarot begins with the Magician and takes us full circle to the World (I'll explain later why the Fool is excluded, so I won't spoil it for you just yet). It's worth noting that the Magician can be depicted either as a young boy (in most decks) or as a mature, austere man (in the Rider-Waite-Smith deck). However, for ease of understanding, we will use the former depiction since it's more commonly used.

Where do we find the Magician in everyday life?

Those who work in commerce or communication, and are often in contact with the public, are well-represented by this card. Magicians know how to speak, sell anything with ease, and navigate through the most challenging situations with elegance and finesse, thanks to their eloquence and savoir faire. Additionally, this card represents people who have a tendency to lie and deceive others.

Level of intensity of the Magician

I would say the Magician ranks a 2 out of 10 in terms of its manageability. Although it is a lovely card when upright, it still requires discipline and direction to fully harness its power. When reversed, although we encounter a lack of enthusiasm or deceit that are quickly exposed, these traits are easily fixed. A mere wave of the wand can restore its positive energies.

The pros of the Magician

Gather around, everybody! A spectacular display is about to unfold, with a tremendous surge of energy waiting to burst out! The Magician card has come out, and it ignites a powerful urge to act, to shine and to demonstrate our full potential. However, we must exercise caution: this boundless energy requires proper guidance, discipline, and direction, or else it could result in chaos. The Magician signifies the start of something new, akin to the youthful phase of a situation. Like a teenager bursting with enthusiasm and ambitions, we must learn to balance this fervor with consistent dedication, knowing when and how to channel it effectively.

The action verb tied to this card is "to dare," which suggests that we are capable of doing anything we set our minds to. The key is to figure out how! In addition to exploring our potential, this card emphasizes the importance of effective communication, which is achieved through cleverness, lightheartedness, intelligence, and humor. When it comes to matters of the heart, this card implies flirtation, newly formed connections, and, since we are in the era of technology, the role of social media in facilitating messaging with a crush or finding a potential mate. Even dating apps are highly recommended, despite some degree of skepticism. One must enter with enthusiasm, but without excessively high expectations. We may find ourselves falling for someone significantly younger or with a youthful spirit. If we are already in a long-term relationship, this card signifies great communication skills between both partners, an unwavering search for enjoyment, and a life filled with adventure and new endeavors. As for career-related inquiries, this card favors new projects and personal initiatives. I highly recommend exploring new opportunities and not idly waiting for a job offer. Use your communication skills during interviews and exams to your best advantage, but don't let boldness get the better of you.

The cons of the Magician

When you take on too many tasks at once, you risk burning out and not accomplishing anything. This is precisely what happens when the Magician card is reversed: our motivation vanishes because we lack direction. We become weak and disinterested, unsure of how to prioritize and start or maintain a project, idea, or relationship. Our best intentions dissipate, leaving us with skills, which we are left unsure of how to use, like an inexperienced and clumsy magician. We struggle to market ourselves because we're unsure of our talents, and we're unlikely to make an impact unless we make a mess of things. If communication is involved, beware of dishonesty, as lies are quickly caught out when this card appears.

In matters of the heart, the reversed Magician card may suggest that the flame of a relationship has lost its spark due because fun and commitment are missing. To rekindle the connection, we must reintroduce the spirit of the early days and organize fun activities. Suspicion of infidelity may also be present, with the card indicating that our trust has been abused by our partner. In such cases, if we choose to consult the Tarot, we must be prepared for what we may learn.

When it comes to our professional lives, we may find ourselves unsure of how to best utilize our talents, and in practice we should start from the basics. We need to identify our strengths and weaknesses, find a balance, and steer our potential in the right direction. If we are lacking a little motivation, simply sitting idle is not an option as this will risk leaving a negative impression and hinder our desired success. If sales-oriented jobs aren't our forte, we can work on improving our public relations skills and learn to excel in our communication skills, becoming a true master of charm. Alternatively, we can explore alternative career paths.

The Magician's advice

"Dear reader, may you indulge in the spectacular performance that lies ahead, for it shall be an experience of grandeur, infused with awe-inspiring surprises and captivating magic. While it may not be perfect, I invite you to have faith in my abilities, and may you leave the show with that same unwavering belief in me. Let us embrace risk-taking and seize this moment without hesitation, for I promise that you shall not regret it!"

A PLAYLIST FOR THE MAGICIAN
Young Folks—Peter Bjorn and John
Promises—The Cranberries
The Wizard—Black Sabbath

SONGS FROM ITALY
Sorridente Truffatore—Amedeo Minghi & Mietta
Il Gatto e la Volpe—Edoardo Bennato
Comprami—Viola Valentino
Mi Vendo—Renato Zero

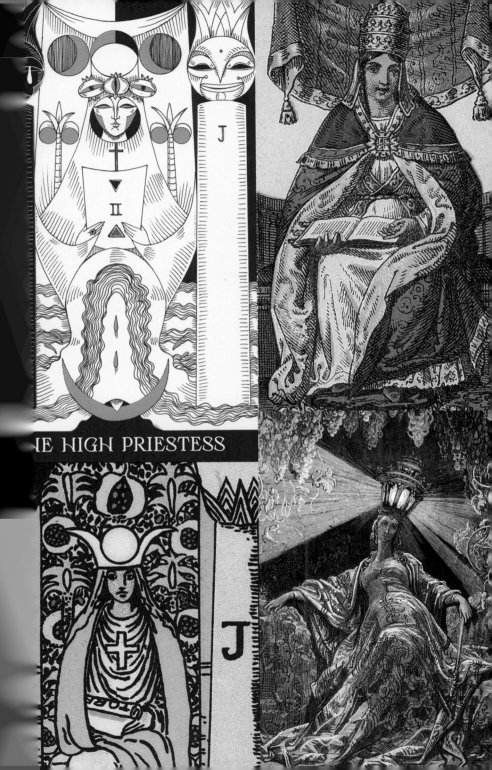

E HIGH PRIESTESS

II · THE HIGH PRIESTESS?
You mean the Log Lady?

Mysterious and distant, the High Priestess captivated us with her icy demeanor, as if she belonged to another world. It's as if she stepped out of a David Lynch movie, embodying the enigmatic allure of Laura Palmer and the profound wisdom of the Log Lady. Do you remember her? If you've watched *Twin Peaks* (and if you haven't, you're missing out! Alice has great recommendations for Tarot, Cinema, and music), you'll surely recall this remarkable character. In Dale Cooper's crucial investigations, she appeared at the most pivotal moments, offering cryptic yet concise advice while cradling her sacred piece of wood. Like the Log Lady, she was rarely seen in public, but those who truly listened and understood her message found her to be an invaluable resource. Similarly, the High Priestess reveals her wisdom through positive Tarot spreads. Are you ready to enter her world, Bae? When you do, make sure you take your shoes off and silently tiptoe around her—she dislikes noise and chatter.

Where do we find the High Priestess in everyday life?

The High Priestess embodies the roles of teachers, therapists, or those with a remarkable talent for listening and guiding us on our personal journeys. These individuals possess the unique ability to provide profound guidance with minimal words. I also think of those who thrive in working alone, fully immersing themselves in their tasks (I must admit, I envy those who possess this skill!). They are people who lead less socially active lives, finding solace in the comfort of their homes, immersing themselves in reading, nurturing their well-being, or cherishing their feline companions. These qualities truly exemplify the essence of the High Priestess. Needless to say, the High Priestess is not one to seek companionship through Tinder or dating apps!

When the High Priestess appears in an unfavorable position, it can indicate individuals who lack spiritual depth and are easily swayed by external opinions or influences. They may speak very little, and when they do, their words often carry a hostile tone. You know the type—the ones who respond with an edgy "NOTHING!" when asked, "What's wrong?" This represents the epitome of the 100% unfavorable energy associated with the High Priestess.

Level of intensity of the High Priestess

The High Priestess is one of those cards that I would categorize as throne holders, where the figures are, as the name suggests, seated on a throne. Its energy is strong and not easily undermined. The aura of silence it radiates demands respect and can be challenging to penetrate. Due to these qualities, I would rate its intensity at 7 out of 10.

The pros of the High Priestess

The appearance of this Major Arcanum signifies the importance of solitude and embracing moments of silence and reflection. The High Priestess is very independent, doesn't need to rely on others to feel complete, often becoming a source of sought-after advice for others. Rather than encouraging immediate action, this card urges contemplation. Therefore, the resolution of the situation in which it appears is likely to unfold slowly. It suggests that projects, ideas, and decisions should be nurtured and carefully considered. Impulsive choices, hasty words, and sudden changes are to be avoided.

For instance, if you wake up one morning with the urge to cut your hair and seek advice from the cards, the presence of this Arcanum indicates the need for reflection to prevent regret over a sudden, unfortunate new hairstyle. In matters of love, if this card appears for someone in a relationship, it signifies individuals who find contentment in their own personal spaces. They do not require constant attachment to experience happiness. Moreover, they tend to be secretive about the details of their bond with the outside world. Further inquiries and card spreads can shed light on whether these qualities extend to all individuals involved in the relationship (as it may not be the case for everyone!).

This card portrays a relationship centered on intellectual connection, built upon mutual understanding. It is characterized by concise communication and profound wisdom. However, it may lack the fiery passion you may have already anticipated.

Is Ms. Betty single and seeking to make new connections? I have my reservations about whether now is the right moment, especially if she hasn't learned to appreciate the value of enjoying life on her own first. This card could convey the message "I dance alone," indicating that she finds great pleasure in spending quality time by herself. To make the most rational use of our intuitions, we need to find ways to filter them and seek concrete feedback from our inner depths. This comes through building experience and applying our intuitive instincts to the practical demands of everyday life. By observing the results we get, we can determine if our feelings are guiding us in a positive direction or if we need to make some adjustments along the way.

The High Priestess is very sensitive to her inner emotions, using them as a guiding compass to navigate life. In the professional field, this skill can be used to connect with our goals and forge our own path without relying on external direction—becoming fully focused and immersed in deep concentration. We also tend to be quite reserved, both in the workplace and when it comes to sharing details about our actions. However, this doesn't mean we are unwilling to offer or receive small pieces of advice related to our work. For those of us who have intuitive abilities, it's crucial to tap into this gift when working on projects or finding solutions. We must think things through independently, without being swayed by external influences, and make choices that align with our inner wisdom.

The cons of the High Priestess

When the High Priestess appears in an unfavorable position, her susceptibility transforms into an overwhelming state of sensitivity. You know that feeling of being constantly on edge? That's precisely what I'm referring to. Excessive stress, absorbing the emotions and aggression of others, can profoundly impact our mood, influenced by the people around us or the environment we find ourselves in. It renders us unapproachable, sometimes leading to feelings of sadness or frustration, which we may express through sharp and harsh words or impenetrable silence that defies investigation. It's as if we want others to pay the price of what they project onto us and the negative energy we absorb from the outside world, even if it has nothing to do with us. This is particularly true when we're grappling with loneliness and suffering.

As you are aware, cartomancy possesses a potent albeit limited power to guide individuals in introspection, but it should never replace proper therapy. When this is the case, I would advise to (discretely) invite Ms. Betty to seek therapy that will allow her to delve deeper into the underlying causes of her stress and the loss of her connection to her inner self. In any case, the prevailing situation is one of profound confusion. The incessant chatter of others' voices fills our ears, attempting to dictate the solutions to our doubts, when, in reality, we should be reestablishing our connection with ourselves and embarking on individual reflections to navigate our own unique paths.

In relationships, there is a prevailing sense of emotional distance and a feeling of being neglected by partners or friends. However, it's important to consider the context of the situation. For Ms. Betty, it's worth reflecting on whether this distance can be resolved or if it's time for her to prioritize self-care. Isolation is particularly challenging, both within and outside of relationships, especially when we struggle to find contentment in our own company. In the workplace, it's important to be mindful of gossip and the potential challenges that come with working independently, especially if we're used to being part of a team. The feeling of being alone can make us feel excluded, disrupt our concentration, and distract us easily. What is it that we're avoiding within ourselves? Why do we constantly seek distractions and divert our attention from what truly matters? Perhaps we just need some time to clear our minds and take a step back—this is the essential message conveyed by this Arcanum.

The High Priestess's advice

"Please, Bae, refrain from speaking unnecessarily just to fill the void with words. Time is a fluid concept; even when it feels scarce, we can learn to create it. Secrets remain hidden until the right moment arrives to unveil them, so let us avoid any gossip until then."

A PLAYLIST FOR THE HIGH PRIESTESS

Enjoy the Silence—Depeche Mode
Silence Is Sexy—Einstürzende Neubauten
Read My Mind—The Killers
Dancing with Myself—Billy Idol
It's Oh So Quiet—Betty Hutton

SONGS FROM ITALY

La Solitudine—Laura Pausini

THE EMPRESS

III · Beyoncé
(I mean THE EMPRESS)

There's a Beyoncé song called "Flawless" where she sings, "I woke up like this, flawless." It's the perfect way to introduce you to the concept of the Empress archetype. When an Empress enters a room, heads turn because she exudes kindness, love, creativity, and captivation. She possesses a maternal and harmonious nature that effortlessly draws people in. It's important to note that she doesn't display superiority over others, in fact, quite the opposite. The Empress embodies all these qualities effortlessly, as it is inherent to her being. Being associated with Venus, she encompasses the characteristics of this planet, which are art, love, beauty, and creativity.

Let's circle back to Beyoncé. She embodies the Empress archetype flawlessly. Beyoncé radiates immense creative energy, effortlessly juggling her roles as a wife, mother, and successful singer, actress, and fashion designer. Her uncanny ability to anticipate trends and her unwavering passion for various forms of art are evident in everything she does. These qualities speak volumes and are a testament to how perfectly she embodies the Empress archetype.

Where do we find the Empress in everyday life?

When we think about professions associated with creativity and beauty, several come to mind: hairdressers, stylists, beauticians, art restorers, graphic designers, illustrators, fashion, or beauty influencers, and those involved in childcare or childbirth. We can also consider that supportive friend who takes care of us after a night of indulgence or suggests a rejuvenating "dinner and skincare" evening to lift our spirits. The Empress archetype also evokes the enchanting image of a geisha, whose literal translation is "person of art," perfectly aligned with the Venusian nature of this card.

Moreover, the Empress represents a loving attitude and the sheer pleasure of engaging in our passions. It encompasses the joy we derive from doing what we love. Conversely, when we encounter this card in reverse, it brings to mind moments when we carry out actions without love or passion, or when our hearts have been shattered, making it challenging to open ourselves up to love again after experiencing disappointment.

Level of intensity of the Empress

The Empress is rated at 3 out of 10—and 3 is also her card number. She brings a sense of ease when she appears in a Tarot spread. She embodies qualities of sweetness and love, encouraging us to sow the seeds of our dreams, which have the potential to blossom into remarkable projects. When the Empress appears in reverse, her demeanor changes from friendly to severe, but beneath that exterior lies a heart that has been broken. It's like a fragile plant in need of tender care and healing, requiring gentle attention, compassion, and nurturing to restore its ability to thrive and flourish once again.

The pros of the Empress

When the Empress card is upright, we embrace the power of love and channel it into the question presented by the person seeking guidance. Dedication and care become paramount in bringing to life a project that holds deep significance for us. Regardless of one's gender identity, this card embodies harmony and a profound connection to our feminine essence, fearlessly embracing its presence. It signifies individuals with heightened sensitivity, who possess a remarkable ability to listen to and understand the struggles of the feminine perspective, providing unwavering support.

When it comes to matters of the heart, the Empress card fosters the growth of new relationships, enabling them to thrive and evolve through intensified emotional bonding and a deep intellectual understanding between the lovers.

This card brings blessings to relationships based on commitment, attraction, sincerity, and a shared desire for common projects. Those lovers enjoy showering their partners with attention, surprises, and creating a loving atmosphere.

If we are not in a relationship, it means we should take care of ourselves and learn self-love and acceptance, including of our physical appearance. Let's focus on giving ourselves the love we deserve instead of relying on someone else to fill our voids in future relationships.

If Ms. Betty asks about the possibility of pregnancy, the presence of the Empress card indicates a positive answer, especially if other cards like the World, the Stars, Temperance, or Judgment also appear in the spread, and all of them are upright. When it comes to work-related questions, if this card appears, it suggests that we are either pursuing our dream profession or finding fulfillment and enjoyment in our current job, becoming passionate about it and finding inspiration every day. It signifies that all the new projects and ideas that arise in our minds are achievable, driven by the Empress's powerful creative energy. And if Ms. Betty aspires to be the next Beyoncé, she certainly has our support and encouragement.

The cons of the Empress

Let's consider the significant impact of climate change on our planet. We witness how droughts and arid conditions lead to agricultural shortages, plants failing to bear fruit, and increasingly severe storms with angrier skies. These are direct consequences of our negligence toward Mother Earth. In this context, we can draw a parallel to the reversed Empress.

The reversed Empress symbolizes the anguish of a love that has ended or remains unrequited. It's the realization that we've invested everything in something that hasn't yielded the desired outcome, resulting in a hardening of our emotions. These contradictions lie at the heart of this Arcanum. We experience a loss of passion, emotional detachment, and a cynical and cold outlook on life, all stemming from deep disappointment. It becomes crucial to understand the underlying causes of these reactions, exploring the individual's life and experiences.

In matters of the heart, the detachment and lack of love can reach such levels that they lead to the breakdown of relationships. In the aftermath of a recent breakup, we seek solace in solitude, finding comfort indulging in ice cream in our pajamas, and perhaps humming "All by Myself" along with Bridget Jones. Healing these wounds requires a focus on self-love.

Single? It often feels like no one we encounter shows any interest. Whether it's failed attempts on dating apps or unsuccessful setups by well-meaning friends, we face a continuous stream of disappointments. Professionally, we may find ourselves stuck in jobs that lack passion and enthusiasm, merely going through the motions without genuine excitement. We forget the beauty of our work, and it becomes essential to rekindle that spark. Alternatively, we can tap into our creative energy and pursue activities that truly ignite our passion. While we may not possess natural artistic talent, with practice, we can incorporate creativity into our lives.

The Empress's advice

"Love unconditionally. Because 'Bae' is also an abbreviation of 'Babe,' a common term of endearment for a loved one, which is what Alice calls the people in her community whom she adores and supports every day. Embrace life as if it were a blooming field, relish its beauty, and strive to become the best version of yourself each day. Allow yourself to fall in love, pursue what brings you joy and fulfillment. Love."

A PLAYLIST FOR THE EMPRESS
Flawless—Beyoncé
Nothing Breaks Like a Heart—Miley Cyrus
Man! I Feel Like a Woman—Shania Twain
Pazzeska—M¥SS KETA feat. Gué Pequeno
Isn't She Lovely—Stevie Wonder
She—Elvis Costello

THE EMPEROR

IV · I've got the Power · THE EMPEROR

There is a song by Beyoncé (who, as you may have guessed, is my favorite artist) called "If I Were a Boy," and its lyrics explore all the things she would do if she were a man. From dressing however she pleases to going out with friends to pursue romantic interests, to prioritizing herself and setting the rules: these are all characteristics of the Arcanum we encounter in this chapter, the Emperor. When we have this card in front of us, we are confronted with a fundamental aspect of our being, which is the ego—a significant and often controversial aspect of a person. If we think about it, many of the adjectives (often viewed negatively) used to describe someone have "ego" as their root: egocentric, egotistical, ego-driven. This is why we sometimes believe that prioritizing others in our lives is a virtuous thing, or we may fear "bothering" others by expressing our own needs and desires. This card teaches us to define who we are, what we want, and what actions we will take to achieve it. And perhaps to embrace that sense of empowerment at least once in our lives, just like that boy in Beyoncé's song.

Where do we find the Emperor in everyday life?

The Emperor is a natural leader, often found in managerial and high responsibility roles. They are the ones who take charge in a company or office, and they may even refer to themselves as an "entrepreneur" on social media. When it comes to making decisions about dinner or vacation, others in their circle tend to follow their lead. This leadership quality creates a small group of followers around them (of course, I'm using some exaggeration here to help illustrate how this card reflects in everyday life).

Now, if we consider the reversed aspects of this card in everyday life, we can think about the phenomenon of incels (involuntary celibates). It's an online subculture that originated in web forums and is predominantly composed of white heterosexual men. These individuals believe that, based on their gender and race, they are entitled to have a romantic partner. However, when they are unable to find a partner, some members of this subculture express their anger and hostility toward women both online and offline. Their beliefs often stem from a distorted sense of male supremacy.

Level of intensity of the Emperor

Dealing with the Emperor can be quite tough, especially when it comes to his less favorable qualities. Picture a powerful figure seated on a throne, displaying unwavering strength. In terms of rating, this card deserves a solid 7 out of 10! Of course, the Emperor would prefer a perfect 10 out of 10, always striving to be the best. However, there are qualities, like indifference, that help bring his grandiosity down a notch.

The pros of the Emperor

The Emperor card symbolizes our personal power and the ability to take charge of our lives. With our full potential expressed, we become aware of our objectives and the means to achieve them. We learn to establish our boundaries and enforce them, without resorting to violence, but rather, by making our opinions known in a clear and confident manner. The Emperor is a natural leader, so embrace his role to make your voice heard.

The Emperor possesses the ability to assert themselves and establish personal boundaries. How does this translate in a reading on matters of the heart? In an existing relationship, it often leads to a natural division of roles where each partner assumes their respective responsibilities and decisions are made harmoniously. This dynamic can also serve as the foundation of the relationship, extending to friendships as well. Some individuals find fulfillment in taking charge and organizing, while others feel more comfortable following and being guided by someone else.

In the flirting phase or when we personally relate to this card, we have the power to take control of the game without waiting for signals from above or the other person. We can approach the object of our desire with confidence. It's worth noting that this card suggests a strong sexual connection, so if you're seeking a casual encounter, it aligns perfectly with that desire. In the professional realm, we have the potential to compete successfully for a promotion or a significant role, showcasing our skills in leadership and management. If we've been dreaming of starting our own business, now is the time to envision this path and create a venture that truly reflects who we are, allowing us to take charge and demonstrate our individual capabilities.

The cons of the Emperor

When the Emperor card appears in a reversed position in a spread, it signifies the disruption of harmony due to toxic power dynamics. This can be observed in individuals who either lack power and desperately seek it, or who are determined to maintain their grip on it. This reversed Arcanum often reveals a significant issue with one's own ego, commonly seen in those who strive to dominate others and harbor a thirst for revenge because they feel cornered and overlooked for too long. Remember, just like the famous line, "Nobody puts Baby in a corner," the Emperor refuses to be subdued. The craving for power knows no bounds!

As with other Arcana, there are two possible interpretations to consider. It's up to you, Bae, to discern which one is most applicable to the situation you are analyzing. When consulting with Ms. Betty, encourage her to embrace what resonates with her and leave the rest behind.

If you approach the reading as an investigative process, seeking feedback as you go along, you will achieve excellent results. Now, let's revisit the scenarios: In the first scenario, we encounter someone (Ms. Betty or the person she seeks information about) who is determined to exert control at any cost. This person may exhibit aggressive, domineering, despotic, and boastful behavior. Their ego is inflated, leading them to feel superior and belittle others. On the other hand, the second scenario is typical of individuals who have always prioritized others, neglecting their own personal power. They occupy minimal space and obediently follow the desires of others.

In relationships, whether they are romantic, friendships, or work-related, the imbalance resulting from these two dynamics can be quite strong. It's essential to be aware of your current state, whichever end of the spectrum you find yourself in. Achieving a balance between the id, the ego, and the super-ego is crucial in establishing our identity, identifying desires, and finding ways to fulfill our needs. Without this balance, we may become extremely impulsive individuals, determined to assert our privileges at any cost, or passive individuals who struggle to articulate their desires and advocate for their needs.

During your conversation with Ms. Betty, it's important to reason with her about the fact that if she doesn't take action for herself, no one else will. Additionally, it's essential to emphasize that shouting and spreading terror are not effective strategies for achieving her desires.

The Emperor's advice

"Bae—I am the force that pitted nations against each other, fueling their thirst for conquest. I am the driving factor behind the brave souls who set sail to explore uncharted territories. I am also the catalyst that will compel you to rise from your seat and approach the person you've been admiring for the past half-hour. I will ignite the fire within you to pursue your deepest desires and instill a sense of pride in your own worth. Embrace me in the appropriate measure, and you shall reap the rewards."

A PLAYLIST FOR THE EMPEROR
If I Were a Boy—Beyoncé
The Power—Snap!
WAP—Cardi B feat. Megan Thee Stallion
Independent Women Part 1—Destiny's Child
Overpowered—Róisín Murphy
Bad Romance—Lady Gaga

THE HIEROPHANT

V · Papa don't preach · THE HIEROPHANT

Sometimes people think I'm younger than I actually am. When I tell them that I feel much older on the inside and that my ideal evening involves staying home with a cozy blanket, watching a movie and dozing off, they look horrified and insist that I'm still young. But deep down, I truly have an old soul, and you know what? I embrace it. This inner sense of old age not only influences my choice of lifestyle in recent years (because, let's be honest, I haven't always felt like an octogenarian on the inside), but it also affects how I organize my work, my love for vintage books, and my appreciation for a nostalgic aesthetic that reminds me of my grandmother's era. I adore wallpapers, doilies, '50s furniture, and vintage clothing. It even seeps into my way of expressing myself, and there's nothing more natural to me than interjecting beloved old sayings. So, when you hear me saying things like "seasons are getting shorter and shorter" or "everything was better back when everything was worse," not only will you hear these sentiments from me, but they are also conveyed by the Hierophant Tarot card, which we are about to explore.

Where do we find the Hierophant in everyday life?

This card is closely associated with the traditions of one's place of birth or country, as well as family hierarchies and religious doctrines. It embodies the wisdom passed down by our grandparents and great-grandparents, who share stories and cherished recipes that have been preserved and handed down through generations, along with our genetic heritage. In education, the Hierophant represents the teachers we encounter on our academic journey, symbolizing the concept of academia itself. We can also see aspects of the Hierophant in those individuals who strive to keep the family unit intact, offering us advice that may seem old-fashioned but still holds value. They take us under their wing, teaching us valuable skills and providing guidance until we're ready to venture out on our own. However, reversed, the Hierophant can signify a false guru, someone who manipulates others with their perceived superiority and uses their influence to control others, similar to the leaders of religious cults.

Level of intensity of the Hierophant

It can be quite challenging to go against the limits imposed by the strict rules of this
card. Considering that the Hierophant (like any reversed card we encounter) represents a powerful energy, its intensity is quite high. Its meaning upright is benevolent and protective, but it also speaks of responsibilities that we may not always
want to take on, which is why I give it a solid 7 out of 10.

The pros of the Hierophant

In real life, the Hierophant—sometimes named the Pope—is a bit like God's personal spokesperson, representing him and conveying his message. He upholds and
celebrates rituals that have remained unchanged for centuries, reflecting Jesus'
Capricorn nature and his appreciation for precision and successful gatherings. He
respects the sacredness of these rituals and expects his followers to do the same.
His followers are like a global family, much like the disciples were for Jesus.

The Church itself has a rigid hierarchical structure, resembling a pyramid, where
each member has a specific role, and all are valuable. In the Tarot, the Pope embodies this role, assuming great responsibility for keeping all the elements involved in
harmony. He is dedicated to preserving tradition and knowledge, bringing order
and stability to the situation.

In Tarot, the Hierophant assumes a similar role, shouldering great responsibility to
maintain harmony and transmit tradition and knowledge. He emphasizes following

established rules and doing things "the right way," discouraging experimentation or excessive daring. When the Hierophant card appears in a reading regarding practical matters, it suggests seeking guidance from someone experienced in that field, someone who can offer valuable advice on how to proceed.

In matters of the heart, the Hierophant symbolizes a preference for traditional values, and its presence indicates that committed relationships can be strengthened through official unions. It encourages individuals to take responsibility for their decisions and urges singles to focus on personal growth before actively pursuing a relationship.

In work-related questions, the Hierophant may represent an authoritative figure who can impart valuable lessons for professional development, as long as their guidance is followed precisely, and work is approached in an orderly and methodical manner. It often pertains to family-run businesses, so it would be worth asking Ms. Betty if this resonates with her.

Additionally, the querent themselves can become a source of protection and guidance for someone else if their experience allows for it.

The cons of the Hierophant

As I mentioned earlier, the Hierophant card values structures and hierarchies. However, when it's reversed, these structures can feel like suffocating cages. We may come across individuals who cling to paternalism and piety, sticking to outdated mindsets that are dull and regressive. Alternatively, it could be the person seeking guidance who displays excessive moralism or suspicion toward anything new.

This card perfectly represents patriarchy, which promotes control and submission of women, hiding behind the guise of preserving traditional gender roles and the integrity of the family. This hinders the independence of women and those who identify as women.

When it comes to the drawbacks of the Hierophant card, as it relates to the individual seeking guidance, they may encounter difficulty in relinquishing control, consistently burdened by guilt over moments they perceive as weaknesses, and find it challenging to embrace new experiences. They have a preference for the familiarity of established routines, even if those routines keep them confined.

The fear of change arises from the perception that it threatens the established system of rules and norms that have been inherited or created as a means of maintaining stability. This system, however, can resemble a gilded cage, limiting personal growth. It can be challenging to break free from this mindset, symbolized by the figure seated on a throne. In relationships, it may indicate a suffocating bond where strict rules are imposed, limiting the other person's freedom. If Ms. Betty is single, she may have high expectations for serious and committed relationships, making it difficult for her to engage in casual dating. This approach may alienate those seeking more casual connections.

In a work setting, if the person seeking guidance finds themselves in a highly structured environment, we can envision someone in a position of authority who acts as an impediment to those under their supervision. They rigidly enforce adherence to established protocols, stifling any creative or innovative attempts. Their expectation is that people unquestioningly accept everything they say as the ultimate truth. It's important to note that Ms. Betty herself may embody these characteristics at times, as she can also play the role of the "perpetrator" in this dynamic.

At the core of this attitude lies the belief that the existing methods are the only valid ones, simply because they have worked to some extent in the past. Unfortunately, this mindset disregards the potential for more promising outcomes that could result from daring ideas. Often, this controlling behavior masks an underlying fear of being overshadowed by emerging technologies or individuals who are more adaptable to changing times. The fear of losing control and power drives their resistance to anything that deviates from the familiar.

On the other hand, if the person seeking guidance works independently, they often find themselves entangled in a myriad of commitments. Their strong sense of responsibility and duty leads them to take on numerous obligations, leaving little room to breathe and confining them within the metaphorical cage I mentioned earlier.

The solution to a reversed Hierophant card lies in challenging the established order, disrupting the rigid structures that hold one back, and inviting a fresh perspective and a sense of freedom into one's life. It involves recognizing that exceptions can coexist alongside rules and embracing the idea that there is flexibility within established frameworks.

The Hierophant's advice

"Listen, remember: If you are able to open your eyes and follow my advice, you can avoid wasting your precious energy. Instead, you'll unlock the potential to reach the same level of brilliance that has endured through time—the past. The future remains uncertain, so it's wise to reflect on the accomplishments of those who came before you, the great ones who have left their mark."

A PLAYLIST FOR THE HIEROPHANT

Papa Don't Preach—Madonna
Coat of Many Colors—Dolly Parton

SONGS FROM ITALY

Ritorno a Casa—Afterhours
Felicità—Albano e Romina Power
Romagna Mia—Raoul Casadei
Le Radici ca Tieni—Sud Sound System

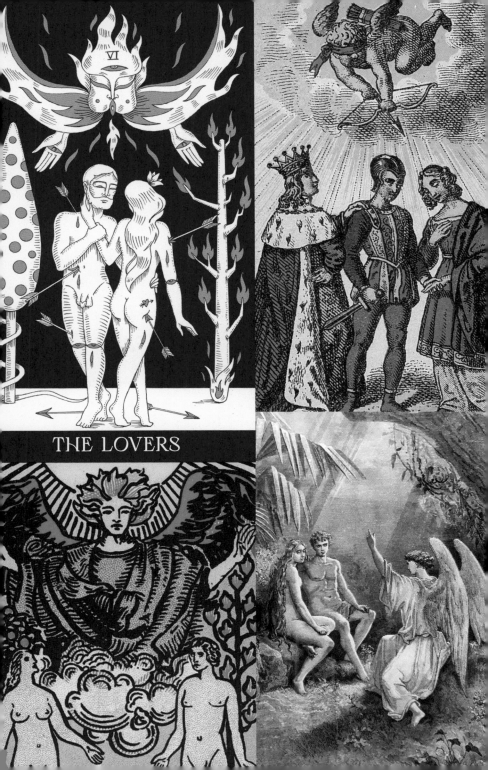

THE LOVERS

VI · THE LOVERS ·
But not romance

Let me make it simple and clear: when the Lovers card appears, it's not about romance or lovey-dovey stuff (unless that's what the question is specifically about). It's actually about making choices, and sometimes we tend to avoid taking responsibility and play the role of a bystander. For example, imagine deciding where to go for dinner with friends. There are those who confidently suggest various options, and then there are those who say, "I'm fine with anything," only to complain later about the chosen place. This card reflects that dynamic, whether it's upright or reversed.

Where do we find the Lovers in everyday life?

If we've encountered people in our lives who are open to exploring different paths before finding the right one, or if we are that kind of person ourselves, it aligns with the essence of the Lovers card in Tarot. It's like having an all-you-can-eat menu where we can try a bit of everything we like or having the freedom to choose our preferred path to reach a destination. Conversely, there are those who constantly struggle with indecision, taking ages to order at a restaurant or feeling torn between their own desires and the expectations of others. Not to mention those who have an "it's my way or the highway" attitude.

Level of intensity of the Lovers

I would rate the Lovers card a solid 7 out of 10. Choosing wisely can be a challenge for us but the potential reward of unlocking new possibilities and moving forward in our endeavors is a strong incentive to embrace this card.

The pros of the Lovers

Personally, I have a deep fondness for the Lovers card because it addresses a fundamental aspect of human life: free will. It encapsulates the concept of our ability to choose between good and bad, without external influence, and taking full responsibility for our decisions. When we actively engage with a situation, we have the power to shape its course based on the choices we make. When this card appears, it suggests that the person seeking guidance may be at a crossroads or faced with multiple options. The key is to discern which choice is the most favorable (though you don't necessarily have to choose only one). The advice here is to act independently of others' interests and the need for approval, not conforming to others' expectations, while still assuming the necessary responsibilities.

As Lady Gaga expresses in her video, "Once you kill the cow, you've got to make the burger," implying that once you've started something, you must follow through. Similarly, we may embark on a certain path, but at some point, we must determine the direction to take and commit to it. In matters of the heart, it's crucial to decide which path to take within a relationship. As the card represents those who tend to be multifaceted, it speaks of a complex individual, perhaps even in matters of love. With this card, there might be a temptation to straddle two boats, to the delight of a partner who doesn't place much emphasis on fidelity, or to maintain a sense of control over the situation. It can also allude to non-monogamous relationships or polygamy, where multiple partners are involved, all consenting and aware of the arrangement.

In work, the Lovers card signifies a plethora of options regarding workplaces, teams, professions, and inclinations. It simply requires careful decision-making, but when the card appears upright, the choice will likely be positive. The surrounding Arcana provide additional insights, with preceding cards indicating the influences that may guide the decision and subsequent cards reflecting the outcome of the chosen option. Typically, when the card is upright, the individual seeking guidance knows how to harmonize their mind and heart, intuition and rationality, enabling them to make positive choices for their future.

The cons of the Lovers

When the Lovers card appears in an unfavorable position, we encounter a familiar situation where the person seeking guidance feels trapped. They may genuinely have no alternatives or are simply allowing themselves to go with the flow without having a say in their own life. It's a passive approach where they tend to follow a predetermined path and settle for what others impose upon them. Another possibility is that Ms. Betty finds herself at the center of a conflict of interests, either self-imposed or orchestrated by someone who is presenting her with a difficult choice.

From an iconographic standpoint, Marseilles decks depict a central male figure faced with a decision between two women representing Vice and Virtue (or three people in some decks). In such situations, it's crucial to take a deep breath and actively make choices for ourselves, preventing others from making decisions on our behalf.

Another aspect highlighted by the Lovers card is indecision or playing both sides, particularly when surrounding cards indicate deception and trickery, such as the Magician or the Moon, both in reverse. For instance, in matters of the heart, indecisiveness regarding choosing a partner can lead to betrayal, causing the person seeking guidance to juggle multiple relationships, resulting in misunderstandings.

When the card is upright, wise choices can be made, but when reversed, there is a risk of betting on the wrong horse (metaphorically, unless you enjoy gambling). It is advisable to carefully consider decisions and reflect before taking action.

The Lovers' advice

"The dilemma is clear: choose or be chosen! Here's a little secret: if you don't make choices in life, you'll end up with whatever scraps are left, and that's usually not much. Think of life as a captivating choose-your-own-adventure book, where your decisions shape the outcome. If you remain stagnant, you'll never discover how your story unfolds. You hold the pen, or perhaps the keyboard, phone, typewriter, or whatever suits you best. It's time to set aside indecision and take control!"

A PLAYLIST FOR THE LOVERS
Should I Stay or Should I go?—The Clash
Hot N Cold—Katy Perry
It's My Life—Bon Jovi

SONGS FROM ITALY
Triangolo—Renato Zero
Pensiero Stupendo—Patty Pravo
Destra-Sinistra—Giorgio Gaber

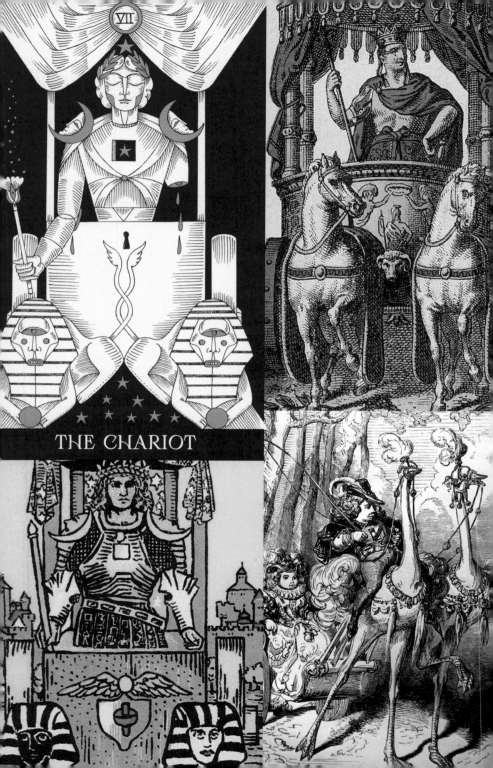

VII

THE CHARIOT

VII · Yes! To traveling · THE CHARIOT

Have you ever played Monopoly? I hope you have because it's one of the most addictive board games out there, and it happens to be my favorite. The reason I mention it is because I believe it holds several analogies to the journey we take through the 22 Major Arcana cards. Just like in Monopoly, there's a starting point, unexpected events, chances, victories, and even some setbacks. After the pause represented by the Lovers card, where we were advised to carefully choose our direction, we kickstart our journey in full throttle with the Chariot. So, fasten your seatbelts and get ready to take plenty of mental notes because one crucial aspect of this card (which, in my opinion, is often overlooked in many Tarot manuals I've come across) is the importance of being able to observe and absorb the world around you as you tread your path of self-realization. It's like the difference between being a mere tourist and a true traveler. Tourists follow a predetermined itinerary, not seeking any adventure or deviating from the plan because their sole focus is reaching the destination. On the other hand, true travelers draw wisdom and growth from each step they take toward their goal. They observe, marvel, and embrace the experiences that surround them, evolving through the journey. Thanks to their open-mindedness, the accomplishment of their goal brings them far more knowledge and fulfillment than they initially anticipated.

Where do we find the Chariot in everyday life?

If you have a passion for traveling or find yourself living as an expat due to educational, work, or personal reasons, then the Chariot card is an excellent fit for you. It encompasses not only physical journeys but also spiritual ones, including the ability to have out-of-body experiences. When we consider the card's transformative nature, it represents those resilient individuals who rise above their difficulties and find the strength to start afresh after experiencing a setback.

Conversely, when the Chariot appears in reverse, it signifies individuals who lack a clear sense of purpose or direction. They move forward without truly assessing the environment they are navigating, which hinders their ability to see the bigger picture and make informed choices.

Level of intensity of the Chariot

In my opinion, encountering the Chariot Arcanum in a reading is truly fascinating. It presents us with the opportunity to confront challenges and embark on a journey of self-discovery, as we actively strive toward a specific goal. Even in moments when it feels like there is no clear direction, the Chariot encourages us to contemplate and navigate our way out of difficult situations. Hence, it doesn't pose significant obstacles, and I would rate its intensity as a moderate 5 out of 10.

The pros of the Chariot

To provide clarity, it is important to distinguish between the practical and metaphorical meanings associated with the Chariot card. These two aspects may not always be integrated into a single interpretation of a question.

Practical meanings: For instance, it could indicate an anticipated relocation that becomes a reality or a long-awaited journey that brings personal benefits. In relationships, it may signify being in love with someone from a different city, country, or culture. The card also encompasses the act of moving, such as considering a change of residence after finding one's dream home. In a work context, the Chariot signifies the potential for a desired transfer or change of location, presenting an opportunity to embrace new challenges. It might even suggest pursuing job opportunities in a different city, resulting in success. Whenever the Chariot card appears, I always suggest that Ms. Betty consider taking a trip, even if it's just for a weekend, to break away from routine and explore new horizons.

Metaphorical meanings: The metaphorical meanings of the Chariot card revolve around love and personal growth. It signifies the possibility of a relationship reaching new heights as both partners strive toward common goals, with the journey itself serving as a continuous source of learning and evolution. If we are currently not in a relationship, it indicates a time to reflect on personal desires and the necessary self-discovery to improve and evolve, both alone and in future partnerships. In a professional setting, it could denote a promotion or the determination to accomplish a personal goal, requiring careful observation of colleagues or competitors. The Chariot card embodies receptiveness, enabling individuals to embrace external influences, absorb knowledge, and utilize them to enrich their lives and foster personal growth.

The cons of the Chariot

When discussing the Chariot card in relation to professionals, it is essential to differentiate between its practical and metaphorical meanings.

Practical meanings: Any physical shifts such as changes in city, workplace, or travel for leisure can present challenges and potentially become problematic. Technical difficulties, for example, might arise during trips. To illustrate, if Ms. Betty is inquiring about a weekend getaway and the Chariot appears in reverse, she should exercise caution in her planning as the trip may not unfold as expected. Subsequent cards following the Chariot will provide further insights into why what was supposed to be a leisurely experience may turn into a weekend of unexpected surprises. For instance, if a reversed Magician card follows, it could indicate that the place she booked is a scam. In matters of relationships, the focus remains on long-distance connections, which often involve complications and difficulties in maintaining relationships across distances. Regarding work-related queries, if Ms. Betty is faced with a move, a business trip, or the need to relocate for job prospects, and she feels uninspired, it is advised to approach the experience with an open mind. It might not turn out entirely negative, and she may discover that the new place offers better opportunities than her current one.

Metaphorical meanings: In matters of love, the Chariot signifies mental distance and the feeling of traveling on separate paths from one's partner. It becomes crucial to assess whether common goals are no longer shared and if the divergence is irreconcilable, or if there is a chance to work toward reconciliation. In professional life, the Chariot represents a lack of direction or goals. It can be a stagnant phase where routines seem futile. An external push may be needed, but it's important to note that not everyone progresses at the same speed, and inspiration doesn't always come from the surrounding environment. It might require introspection to find the necessary stimulus or to reassess aspirations. It's important to honestly evaluate whether pursuing a position in that particular field is truly what one desires. Sometimes, goals need to be revised on a personal level as well. There may be an assumption that pursuing a specific path or half-hearted commitment is the "norm," which can lead to performance anxieties or feelings of inferiority, causing internal barriers. Setting more attainable and relatable goals that feel within reach can help overcome such obstacles and provide a sense of accomplishment.

The Chariot's advice

"Rather than purchasing postcards, capture moments through photographs. Instead of opting for hotels, embrace the hospitality of locals. A true journey should be lived to its fullest, not merely for the purpose of showcasing little flags planted across different corners of the globe, but to genuinely absorb the enriching experiences it offers. The true value lies in personal growth attained through each destination, far more significant than returning home with a suitcase filled with plastic souvenirs."

A PLAYLIST FOR THE CHARIOT
Take Me Home, Country Roads—John Denver
Ride—Lana Del Rey
Voyage, Voyage—Desireless
Nowhere to Go—Hayden James feat. Naations

SONGS FROM ITALY
Sì, Viaggiare—Lucio Battisti
Samarcanda—Roberto Vecchioni

STRENGTH

VIII · STRENGTH lies not in mere muscle

"Power is nothing without control." This memorable slogan originated from a famous tire commercial back in the 90s, a time when commercials truly knew how to captivate. While it's unlikely that the creator of this slogan drew inspiration from the Tarot card, it unexpectedly serves as a perfect introduction to this card's essence. Allow me to elaborate: the Tarot card of Strength delivers a profound message, highlighting the significance of motivation, self-control, and kindness over sheer physical force. In the traditional depiction, a tranquil scene unfolds, depicting a woman effortlessly holding the jaws of a lion, which futilely attempts to resist. Serenity graces the woman's face, evoking a sense of ease as if she were taming a cuddly teddy bear. It projects a peaceful vibe, without any violent or aggressive elements. This peaceful representation conveys that nonviolence, courage, gentleness, and wit possess the potential to conquer our own animalistic instincts as well as those of others.

Where do we find Strength in everyday life?

I associate this Arcanum with tireless individuals, even in sweltering heat. It pertains to those who train themselves to have their minds conquer their bodies, like the dedicated fitness instructors who inspire and push their clients to surpass their physical limits. It also encompasses those who skillfully handle diverse family dynamics while juggling their work responsibilities, such as single parents.

Level of intensity of Strength

It's always nice to have energy resources ready to be used, but they alone are not sufficient. It's important to use our intellect to know how to channel that energy effectively. At the same time, if our physical strength doesn't support our willpower, we won't make much progress. I would rate Strength as a 7 out of 10 in terms of intensity, especially because our energy often runs out quickly.

The pros of Strength

This card brings a real surge of strength to the person seeking guidance. It empowers them to invest their energy, both mentally and physically, into the matter at hand. It's a great moment where the mind and body align to achieve a set goal, fueled by determination, persuasive abilities, and personal integrity.

In relationships, it signifies the capacity to support loved ones and nurture bonds with persistence and determination, be it in a romantic or platonic connection. If Ms. Betty is seeking information about a new acquaintance, there may be a strong intellectual connection alongside the obvious mutual attraction. The relationship can become lively, driven not only by physical chemistry but also by a shared desire for intellectual growth.

When facing challenges, negotiating, or fighting personal battles, success lies in overcoming fears, showing courage, and taking a diplomatic approach rather than resorting to aggression. Speaking from the heart and having a gentle touch can even melt the most resistant of barriers.

Even in challenging circumstances, our genuine intentions and noble demeanor can unravel the most complex situations. We must roll up our sleeves, employ strategic thinking, and take action to achieve our desired outcomes. This card exudes immense energy, allowing us to overcome obstacles without feeling drained. However, it's crucial to recognize that energy levels fluctuate, and knowing when to rest and slowdown is just as important.

The cons of Strength

Take a moment and listen to your body, Bae. What is it trying to tell you? Is it urging you to slow down? Is it struggling to keep up with your mind? It's time to prioritize self-care because you're running on empty, and soon you'll run out completely. Your energy was meant for something significant, but when faced with strong opposition, there's nothing left to draw from, and that's why you feel exhausted and overwhelmed by life.

First and foremost, try to avoid unnecessary conflicts. Before you unleash your inner Gordon Ramsay and start shouting and lashing out, take a deep breath. Think as clearly as possible. If you're feeling weak, simplify your lifestyle and don't attempt to juggle multiple tasks at once. Accept that you can't do it all and conserve your energy.

This card is a signal that it's time to replenish yourself. Take supplements, engage in positive activities for your body, whether it's getting a good night's sleep or treating yourself to a spa day. In relationships, it indicates that after giving your all (and perhaps doing more than your fair share), it's time to reassess and prioritize your own happiness. If the effort is imbalanced and you're overextending yourself, it's easy to reach a point of feeling completely drained. This card doesn't necessarily signify the end of a relationship, but it's an opportunity for Ms. Betty to consider if the effort is still worthwhile.

In the professional field, my best advice is to request time off, seek support, and delegate tasks—anything to conserve energy and keep going. Rest is crucial; don't push yourself beyond your limits. You've lost your motivation, the driving force that made you feel invincible. Take a vacation, trust me, and reconnect with your inner drive to pursue your personal mission once again.

Strength's advice

"I'm relentless, constantly multitasking, and I'll captivate you with my cunning tactics. But I can quickly run out of steam, so don't forget to recharge me regularly if you don't want to feel abandoned when you least expect it."

A PLAYLIST FOR STRENGTH
Eye of the Tiger—Survivor
Strong Enough—Cher
Soldier—Destiny's Child
Fighter—Christina Aguilera

SONGS FROM ITALY
La Leva Calcistica della Classe '68—Francesco de Gregori
Coraggio, Onestà e Lealtà—Carmen Consoli

IX

THE HERMIT

IX · Sean Connery · THE HERMIT

Take a moment to hold the Hermit card in your hand and reflect on its message. It has always reminded me of Sean Connery's character in *The Name of the Rose*. When I consider the vibes Connery brings to that film and the story itself, I find that they align well with some of the meanings of this card.

Firstly, there's the theme of solitude. The Hermit represents a period of introspection and self-reflection. Secondly, there's the pursuit of truth, a central element in the movie's plot. The story unfolds within the confines of a monastery, which, in my imagination, is often secluded from the outside world. And of course, there's the uncovering and solving of a mystery, which resonates with the Hermit's symbolism.

Among the various connections I draw between Tarot and popular culture references, this one feels particularly fitting.

Where do we find the Hermit in everyday life?

This card can represent those who play a role in improving our physical and/or psychological well-being. Think of yoga or meditation instructors, as well as professionals who help alleviate physical discomfort like osteopaths and physiotherapists. It can also symbolize grandparents and grandmothers, especially those who have experienced the loss of a spouse. Additionally, it encompasses individuals who live on the edges of society, whether by choice or circumstance, holding onto a personal truth that goes beyond our perception or understanding. We're referring to the homeless, ascetics, and *Hikikomori*, among others.

Level of intensity of the Hermit

I would rate it at least 8 out of 10 in terms of significance. This card represents qualities such as maturity, the capacity to express our deepest emotions, and having a thick skin. Even when upright, it holds a challenging energy.

The pros of the Hermit

One of the strengths of this Arcanum is its ability to see beyond surface-level appearances and delve deep into the heart of the matter indicated by the question. However, achieving this requires more than just impulsive actions or spontaneous decisions. It calls for wisdom and, most importantly, patience. If you often find yourself rushing through things without much thought or constantly feeling overwhelmed, then this card is meant for you. It can guide you toward finding tranquility and help you discern what truly holds value in life. And here's a little spoiler: it's not material possessions.

The Hermit invites you to shed unnecessary layers and seek out the essence of life, the things that are invisible to the naked eye, as beautifully depicted in *The Little Prince*. It encourages you to embrace solitude as a path to self-discovery, to detach yourself from worldly distractions, and to find contentment in simplicity. In the realm of relationships, this card suggests the importance of maintaining individuality and personal space, allowing each person to pursue their own interests without feeling neglected or abandoned. And if you're currently single, it's a reminder that this is a time for self-reflection rather than seeking romantic involvement. Let's embrace the value of solitude, stand confidently on our own two feet, and embark on a journey of self-growth to uncover our true desires (and if anyone figures it out, do share your insights with us!).

When it comes to work, this card represents growth. We acquire knowledge, working diligently and quietly, just like those famous Benedictine monks from *The Name of the Rose*. Some see us as highly skilled in our field, granting us the freedom to work independently. If we realize that our professional destiny lies in self-employment, we approach it calmly, having experienced teamwork and realizing that the "#dreamteam" hashtag isn't our thing. On a personal and emotional level, we go through a transition from one phase of life to another, often being asked to shoulder more responsibility and maturity than our age might suggest. The Hermit serves as a spiritual detox: we seek truth, understand what truly matters, and take care of it.

The cons of the Hermit

In Italy, we have a renowned singer named Laura Pausini, who performed a song called "La Solitudine" at the Sanremo music festival. The title translates to "Loneliness." It's understandable that loneliness frightened young Laura, considering she was only 18 years old and had much growing up to do.

When the Hermit card is reversed, it can manifest in two distinct ways. Firstly, the individual tends to isolate themselves to an extreme degree, struggling to maintain social connections. Their personal neglect takes on a darker significance than that of the Empress. This extreme isolation is exemplified by the Japanese term "hikikomori," which literally means "standing apart." It refers to individuals, often adolescents, who never leave their rooms, even for meals, opting for complete withdrawal from society.

In the second case, however, to avoid being alone, Ms. Betty surrounds herself with circumstantial friendships, engaging in relationships based on opportunism. Have you heard of FOMO? This acronym stands for "Fear Of Missing Out," representing the anxiety of potentially missing out on important social events and being excluded from socializing. This fear can lead individuals to overindulge in activities or outings simply to avoid being alone.

As for relationships, Ms. Betty yearns for companionship but struggles to fulfill this desire. She perceives loneliness as a looming threat and fails to find any positive aspects within it. Even simple pleasures like lounging in her underwear, singing along to the Spice Girls while attending to her beauty routine, do not alleviate the negative feelings. The unfavorable depiction of the Hermit card can also signify a fear of aging, indicating a need for intervention and self-care.

If a relationship is already underway, as exemplified by the High Priestess card, the individual may feel undervalued by their partner. They may start believing that they are unimportant or that their personal story holds no significance. In the professional world, there is a risk of isolation. If someone is attempting to sideline us, certain cards may indicate traps or a hostile work environment (such as the reversed Magician, reversed Moon, or reversed Temperance cards).

It's possible that the assigned job demands greater responsibilities than our current capabilities or requires working independently, which may not be a suitable fit for us. On a personal level, we may have lost sight of our true path, becoming excessively distracted by trivial and superficial matters or relationships. We fail to delve deeply into important matters, instead acting impulsively or without a strategic plan.

The Hermit's advice

"Take it slow and steady, and you'll make remarkable progress while maintaining your well-being. Start crafting your journey of self-improvement to the rhythm of your favorite playlist. It may feel like resources are limited, but incredible accomplishments have come from humble beginnings. Look deep within your heart and discover the true essence of things. The answers you seek reside within you. If you'd like, jot them down in your journal for future reference. And always remember, there are moments when it's wiser to be alone than simply to settle for companionship."

A PLAYLIST FOR THE HERMIT
Isolation—Joy Division
Hikikomori—Willie Peyote
Better Off Alone—Alice DeeJay

SONGS FROM ITALY
Piazza Grande—Lucio Dalla
Io, Vagabondo—I Nomadi
E ti Vengo a Cercare—Franco Battiato

THE WHEEL

X · Spin, spin! It's THE WHEEL OF FORTUNE!

Just mentioning the Wheel of Fortune Tarot card instantly evokes memories of one of the most iconic TV game shows from the 70s. Game shows like *Wheel of Fortune* have left a lasting imprint on our collective memory, including the enthusiastic cheers of the audience, hoping to bring luck to each contestant in turn. This concept of a wheel associated with games and luck is a recurring theme. Consider the famous casino game roulette, where the circular wheel symbolizes the perfect accompaniment to chance, conveying fortune and winnings. Humans have always been captivated by circular forms, and the Wheel of Fortune extends beyond being just a Tarot card or a captivating TV program. It holds an allegorical significance that gained popularity in writings and illustrations since the late Middle Ages. Depicting the blindfolded goddess Fortuna spinning a wheel, the powerful figures of that time clung to it, as it granted them either success or misfortune in a completely arbitrary manner, depending on the force exerted during the spin. Since then, its cyclic nature and the unpredictable nature of its favor has inspired novels, songs, and even a *Magic: The Gathering* card, where its appearance forces all players to discard their hand and draw seven new cards at random.

Where do we find the Wheel of Fortune in everyday life?

I often find myself reflecting on the twists of fate that have the power to unexpectedly shape our lives. It's like those moments when we happen to be in the right place at the right time. Like that stroke of luck that allows us to catch a flight or train just in the nick of time. In our everyday lives, the Wheel of Fortune can be likened to pleasant surprises like finding money on the ground, entering into favorable marriage, or winning prize competitions. Especially when it comes to finances, it holds the potential to unleash an exciting wave of unexpected good fortune

Level of intensity of the Wheel of Fortune

The Wheel has the power to grant or to withhold: its unpredictability can bring both joy and despair, depending on how it presents itself. It is this very quality that makes it difficult to define as easy or hard, so it could be anything from 1 to 10 out of 10!

The pros of the Wheel of Fortune

Whether this card represents you or Ms. Betty, it signals that luck is on your side in the current situation. When the Wheel of Fortune appears favorably, it suggests a readiness to make positive things happen, as we become more open to the opportunities that come with good fortune. If you've been through a tough period, seeing this card in a spread means you're leaving that cycle behind and can look forward to better times ahead.

In matters of the heart, it can indicate shared investments that contribute to the well-being of the relationship, like buying a house, a car, or going on a trip. Generally, it's a good time for romantic relationships, as you enter a phase full of pleasant surprises. If you've been on a date and wonder if there will be another, the answer is likely yes.

In the workplace, projects and collaborations you seek will prove rewarding, and if you're thinking of asking for a raise, this card bodes well for success. Sales and investments are also favored, bringing a substantial boost to your finances. If you've made thoughtful choices, the outcomes will be positive and swift, as the Wheel represents a sudden shift from a low to a high. So, my advice with this card is to seize the moment and enjoy the ride. Grab that opportunity before it passes you by!

The cons of the Wheel of Fortune

In an unfavorable position, this card can be summed up with one word: misfortune. It could be the result of past poor choices now manifesting their consequences, or it might be a temporary period where fate seems to be testing us with a series of unfortunate events. What we should avoid is acting impulsively or seeking temporary refuge while feeling defeated. Instead, we should focus on learning from this experience and striving for better outcomes in the next cycle. It's possible that a missed opportunity has led to a dry spell, simply because we lacked the courage to seize our chance when it presented itself. To get a clearer picture of what could go wrong with the unfortunate Wheel, it's helpful to consider the subsequent cards. As a card symbolizing movement, its opposite effect can leave us feeling stagnant and trapped in a kind of limbo. In terms of relationships, we might find ourselves nearing the end of a cycle, perceiving it in a pessimistic light as if misfortune has befallen us. If we had hopes of reconnecting with someone from the past, it's unlikely to happen. We can choose to wallow at home, indulging in ice cream on the couch, or we can wipe away our tears and focus on the future. There are plenty more fish in the sea!

At work, we may have experienced a negative change in position or faced a string of unfortunate events. In such times, it's important not to rush into decisions to fix things hastily. Instead, let's take a step back and honestly reflect on why these challenges are happening. Is there anything we can take responsibility for, or is it an external factor beyond our control? It's also helpful to consider the bigger picture and realize that these hardships could potentially lead to better outcomes in the future. While it may be difficult to see now, these tough moments are temporary and part of a larger puzzle. Even setbacks teach us valuable lessons about how the world works. So, let's stay strong, learn from these experiences quickly, and be cautious with our finances. It's wise to avoid risky investments, even if it involves tempting luxury items like a Birkin bag.

The Wheel of Fortune's advice

"Come closer and give me a good spin! I'm like a dice game or a lucky hand in poker. Strategy isn't always enough to win, sometimes you also need a good bit of luck! But you'll never know if you don't try!"

A PLAYLIST FOR THE WHEEL OF FORTUNE
Hymn of the Big Wheel—Massive Attack
What Goes Around… Comes Around—Justin Timberlake
Ironic—Alanis Morissette
Ka-Ching!—Shania Twain
Wheel of Fortune—Ace of Base

SONGS FROM ITALY
Ricchi Per Sempre—Sfera Ebbasta

JUSTICE

XI · JUSTICE · Growing up with judge and jury tv shows

When I was little, not so long ago (wink, wink), one of my favorite things to do when I had to stay home from school with a fever was to enjoy my ultimate comfort food—a warm, hearty bowl of soup. And what made it even better was watching the Italian equivalent of *Judge Judy* and other court TV shows. The storylines were captivating, sometimes silly, but what fascinated me the most was the High Judge herself. I absorbed her words and opinions, forming my own ideas about what was right and wrong. It was like I was becoming my own little legal expert. That experience was my first glimpse into understanding justice, and it's a trait I still greatly admire today. I know life isn't always as simple as black or white, and there are nuances in between, but I firmly believe that those who take advantage of others should not be rewarded. Maybe I've watched one too many superhero movies! This same sense of justice is embodied in the Justice Arcanum, which is why it holds a special place in my heart. It's a mechanism that rewards those who live by fair standards, even though I'm far from being a saint—which brings to mind the lyrics of an Italian song—"I'm Not a Saint, I'm Just a Woman"—well, that's me! With that said, let's dive into what this Arcanum represents.

Where do we find Justice in everyday life?

It may seem obvious, but when we interact with lawyers, notaries, accountants, and politicians (always hoping for their honesty), we essentially come face to face with the embodiment of justice in human form. Moreover, the dynamics surrounding these professions also mirror the essence of the Justice card. Think about complaints, bills, taxes, contracts, and a range of disputes, including personal conflicts. In our day-to-day lives, justice can take the shape of someone we frequently turn to for mediation or to bring peace to discussions, thanks to their impartiality. On the other hand, I can't help but think of Chick Calimero and his famous line, "It's an injustice!" Now, my dear reader, I am old-fashioned, and I remember Calimero on TV, but if you happen to belong to Generation Z and are unfamiliar with this chirpy little character, make sure you google it!

Level of intensity of Justice

We begin with the assumption that when we encounter a figure seated on a throne, we are faced with a rather formidable energy to unravel. I refer to these Arcana as the throne holders—the regal figures who exude a commanding presence, encompassed by an aura that is both intimidating yet benevolent when reversed, or formidable and challenging to navigate when upright. For this very reason, I assign Justice a level of intensity at 8 out of 10. If it appears in a favorable position, it presents us with a stimulating challenge, aligned with our interests. However, when in an unfavorable position, it can prove tricky to contend with.

The pros of Justice

Every action has a consequence. When it is driven by goodwill, there is a significant likelihood of achieving a positive outcome. This fundamental principle is embodied in the Justice Arcanum. If Justice were an influencer, she would proudly sport a t-shirt that reads, "It's Karma, Bitch." Through this card, we gain profound insights and learn from our own experiences, enabling us to rectify mistakes and stay true to the path of righteousness. Assuming that you have conducted yourself appropriately, the appearance of the Justice card signifies that your conduct is being rewarded. It indicates that the environment in which you have immersed yourself shares the same system of values, perspectives, and morals, endorsing your actions favorably. On an emotional level, it represents stability, reliability, and a balanced disposition—not prone to intense passionate or romantic outbursts, but rather grounded in fairness.

Since this card pertains to contracts, if we seek guidance from the Tarot regarding the course of a romantic relationship and the Justice card appears, it may be worth considering the notion of marriage. What does this card reveal in terms of work? Let's consider the example of Ms. Betty at a recruitment day for a position she has applied for. With Justice, there is a strong possibility that she will pass it. Additionally, the contracts she signs in her workplace are reliable and trustworthy. The presence of a high moral standard fosters an environment where she can work with serenity, free from the fear of dismissal. On the other hand, if Ms. Betty has filed a lawsuit against her employer, Justice assures her victory because she stands on the side of righteousness. Justice also highlights the significance of feeling understood by the individuals who share our values, creating an atmosphere where judgment is absent, and we are not made to feel wrong.

The cons of Justice

When the Justice card is reversed, we need to consider whether we are engaging in fraudulent behavior or if the other party is. It's because someone is playing dirty and believes they can get away with it. However, as they say "what goes around, comes around" and sooner or later, everything will catch up with us. If Ms. Betty hasn't been conducting herself in the best of manners, the reversed Justice card indicates that the repercussions of her actions will unfold accordingly. This applies not only to personal matters but also to practical situations such as unpaid bills or taxes. It's better to address these issues to avoid unpleasant surprises in the future. In love, the feeling of not being understood can lead to a breakup, or if married, to a separation or divorce. One party has undoubtedly experienced some sort of injustice, prompting the need for deeper investigation to uncover any instances of betrayal. As for the rest of our relationships, if the Justice card is reversed, it suggests the likelihood of arguments stemming from misunderstandings. It becomes challenging to find a resolution when the person who initiated the conflict is unwilling to reconsider their position. It is crucial to seek guidance from someone we can trust to help us decide whether it is worth persisting in our pursuit or if it's time to reevaluate our friendship. The desire for approval is a central theme of the reversed Justice card. We frequently seek validation to feel a sense of belonging and acceptance among our relationships. Yet, when approval is missing and our unique ideas make us appear rebellious, it becomes challenging to overcome the feeling of being disconnected from prevailing moral norms. We must foster self-assurance and take comfort in our choices, even if others struggle to comprehend or show little inclination to bridge the gap between our perspectives and theirs. It is natural for us to desire validation within our social circles, as it allows us to feel connected and valued. However, when we find ourselves excluded from approval or labeled as rebels due to our differing ideas, it becomes challenging to overcome the sense of not fitting into the prevailing moral norms and standards. In these circumstances, embracing our rebellious nature can serve as an empowering remedy. It is crucial for us to nurture self-confidence and find comfort in our choices, even when others struggle to understand us. It is essential to be careful when it comes to dismissals at work. We should think about whether our behavior might have played a part in any repercussions, whether we have been targets of mistreatment, or both. Consulting unions or legal professionals may be a good approach to address any prejudice or to ensure our rights are safeguarded.

Justice's advice

"Everything in life can be a double-edged sword, with the power to destroy or to nurture. But it all comes down to how we handle it. When you strive to act with integrity, fear loses its hold on you. If you ever find yourself in need, take this sword from me. Think of it as a tool to carve away any unwanted aspects from your life. Just remember to be cautious and not carry it with you all the time, as it could breed complications. Instead, consider your choices and their consequences carefully, and aim for fairness in everything you do."

A PLAYLIST FOR JUSTICE
Karma Police—Radiohead
New Rules—Dua Lipa
Not Fair—Lily Allen
Minority—Green Day

SONGS FROM ITALY
Nessuno Mi Può Giudicare—Caterina Caselli
Un Giudice—Fabrizio De André

THE HANGED MAN

XII · THE HANGED MAN · Don't leave me hanging

I shouldn't show a preference for specific Major Arcana cards because it might seem like I appreciate the others less. We understand that to be well-rounded individuals, we need to experience all 22 cards of the Tarot and embrace life in all its diverse shades. However, I can't help but confess my deep fondness for the Hanged Man, even though it may be a somewhat controversial card. From a spiritual perspective, the Hanged Man is truly remarkable. It symbolizes letting go of all worldly attachments and a complete immersion into spirituality and the unknown. It encourages us to let go of preconceived ideas and embrace new perspectives. This is symbolized by the fact that the Hanged Man is typically depicted upside down. Despite his seemingly uncomfortable position, his serene expression reminds us to accept our circumstances. It is intriguing to note the resemblance between the state depicted by the Hanged Man and the practice of bondage, which is a practice of BDSM. In bondage, individuals who are tied up or suspended may find pleasure in the restriction or temporary limitation of their movements, experiencing a state of complete passivity and surrender to discomfort. Reflecting on the Hanged Man, it embodies qualities of great generosity and selflessness. The Hanged Man card is also perfect for those who have a desire to explore or study the esoteric world. Individuals who sacrifice everything for the well-being of others or wholeheartedly devote themselves to caregiving face the potential risk of losing sight of their own needs and fail to maintain a proper balance. It is indeed a delicate balance to strike.

Where do we find the Hanged Man in everyday life?

I associate this card with anyone who works in a field that involves caring for people, such as carers, nurses, or social workers. Additionally, those who do volunteer work, as well as mediums and clairvoyants who offer their abilities to aid investigations, can be seen as the embodiment of the Hanged Man. People who are willing to help an elderly person cross the street or carry groceries for them, as well as the friend who is always there in times of need, also come to mind. If you believe in mutual aid and your nature is generous, you are the Hanged Man! Unfortunately, often individuals with a giving spirit are taken advantage of as they seldom seek anything in return for their assistance.

Level of intensity of the Hanged Man

The Hanged Man card imparts valuable lessons on sacrifice, patience, and the occasional state of involuntary passiveness. It is a challenging card, deserving an impressive 8 out of 10 rating in terms of difficulty!

The pros of the Hanged Man

Take a deep breath, surrender to the stillness, and embrace the art of waiting, my dear reader. In this moment of your profound journey toward self-realization, you have consciously paused the relentless pursuit of filling the void with hurried actions. Instead, you have chosen the path of meditation and reflection. The ability to step back, to make a sacrifice if you will, for the sake of a greater good, is not in vain. Rest assured, the rewards shall come, though perhaps not immediately. They will arrive in due time. "How long must I wait?" you may wonder. Alas, I cannot provide a definitive answer, for everything seems to be on hold. However, I urge you not to remain idle with your hands tucked away in your pockets. Instead, seize this opportunity to study your next move, envision a strategy, and nurture the seeds of a project that shall blossom as soon as you are released from the constraints that bind you.

From the outside, this card may appear somewhat static and uneventful. However, the true transformation it represents takes place within, much like the unseen progress of a pregnancy or the behind-the-scenes process of baking a cake. Achieving our desires requires patience and avoiding actions that could jeopardize the desired outcome.

In relationships, the Hanged Man does not bring immediate excitement or significant changes, but rather, it signals a need for reflection and contemplation. If we are anticipating responses or signs of life from others, we must be prepared for a delayed response. On the other hand, if we are the ones who need to take action, we should be patient and wait until we feel ready to make our move.

If we are single, with nothing in particular on the horizon, it is important to prioritize our own needs and desires. Otherwise, we run the risk of accommodating others excessively and potentially become a bit of a rescuer. As for relationships, this card doesn't indicate any particular sexual energy. In both our professional and personal lives, we often encounter frustrating delays in getting responses or receiving payments. On the other hand, we might find ourselves putting in a lot of effort in a job that brings us fulfillment but doesn't quite pay the bills. It's crucial to carefully weigh whether these endeavors are truly worthwhile. Take, for example, internships that offer meager expense reimbursement. They can be a stepping stone to exciting projects or companies that align with our values and have the potential to open doors to future opportunities. While it may involve making a small sacrifice, we hope that it will ultimately lead to significant results. I'd like to point out that this card is very promising when it comes to spiritual matters as it indicates our ability to fully embrace the spiritual realm.

The cons of the Hanged Man

Attempting to disentangle oneself or alter an unfavorable situation while suspended in the position of the Hanged Man is an exercise in futility. It represents a state where circumstances prevent any meaningful change or progress. You feel trapped and unable to move in any direction, as if others benefit while you remain stuck in discomfort. The constraints of the situation leave little room for maneuvering, and the mental clarity needed to explore alternative solutions or devise strategies for the future is elusive. It's worth noting that the Hanged Man, whether upright or reversed, often emerged during the pandemic lockdown period, symbolizing the collective feeling of being stuck and uncertain about the way forward. While some individuals found ways to make the most of this period, others faced challenges—everyone's resilience is unique, and everyone did their best with the resources they had available.

Just like the appearance of this card, everything depends on the strength of our mindset to confront a particular situation where we feel constrained and trapped. Sacrifice becomes necessary whenever this card appears. It's crucial to handle our finances with caution, as it indicates a challenging relationship with money, often leading to overspending or an inability to save what we earn. It also highlights how everyday expenses can exacerbate our financial struggles. I suggest being mindful of expenses, saving money, and refraining from excessive generosity, such as treating others to dinners and snacks, solely based on our kind-hearted nature.

The Hanged Man, with its Neptunian energy, is closely associated with dreams and ideals. It represents those who tend to be a bit narrow-minded and unable to see the bigger picture. I mention this because sometimes we feel pressured to take a backseat and play a supporting role, sacrificing our own interests for the benefit of others. But is that really the case? Are we truly unable to make decisions, or do we simply hope that someone will reward us for doing nothing?

Let's consider Ms. Betty as an example. She's been pushed aside by her partner and is waiting for their return. Or perhaps she's waiting to sell her house, lowering the price because the real estate agent is not a proactive seller. Is it really wise to advise her to wait for others to take the initiative? If she opens her eyes, she might realize that she has the power to break free from her partner's hold or find a more proactive real estate agency. Who knows? In the meantime, let's try to help her see the importance of not waiting around and taking charge of her own decisions, independent of the expectations and timelines imposed by others.

The Hanged Man's advice

"You can see things differently with just a small change. Sometimes, try looking at things from a different angle, like upside down. Break free from fixed ideas or beliefs, but take care! Handstands aren't for everyone!"

A PLAYLIST FOR THE HANGED MAN
Waiting Room—Fugazi
Ladies and Gentlemen We Are Floating in Space—Spiritualized
Fix You—Coldplay
Where Is My Mind?—Pixies

SONGS FROM ITALY
Liberato—Me Staje Appennenn' Amò
La Cura—Franco Battiato

DEATH

XIII · DEATH · The forbidden word

"Passed away," "passed on," "no longer with us"—there are so many different ways to express such a straightforward concept. What about just "dead," Bae? It's as simple as that. Or is it? Why is death still considered a taboo in the Western world? If you think about it, even Voldemort, whose name literally hides the word "Mors" ("Death" in Latin), can't be mentioned! And just like the card we're looking at now, in some decks it doesn't even have a name, only the number XIII is shown. The concept of death and passing away definitely involves pain, but what is it that really scares us about this card? Is it the name itself or what lies behind its meaning? Removing nonessential parts of our existence, making changes, and leaving a piece of ourselves behind are processes that resemble grieving. But as the lyrics of Caterina Caselli—an Italian singer—go, "You must die a little to be able to live." I can assure you that once you finish reading this chapter on the Arcanum XIII, it won't frighten you anymore!

Where do we find Death in everyday life?

This Arcanum can be likened to the transitions between different stages of life, such as the process of the Saturn return in astrology. It's when our natal Saturn returns to the same sign it occupied when we were born, marking our entry into adulthood (usually around age 29). Individuals who frequently reinvent themselves, those passionate about or working in esoteric realms, and those who make transformative changes to overcome obstacles embody the positive aspects of Death. On the other hand, the negative aspects pertain to individuals who remain fixated on the past, trapped in stagnant situations, or burdened by unresolved issues they cannot put to rest.

Level of intensity of Death

Letting go of what no longer serves us or undergoing a personal transformation by giving our lives, or even ourselves, a makeover can be incredibly rewarding. However, it requires the right mindset to take that step, as reaching for the big scary scissors is not a decision to be taken lightly. In my view, the intensity of Death is about an 8 out of 10.

The pros of Death

Do you recall the famous quote by Lavoisier? And, more importantly, are you familiar with Antoine-Laurent de Lavoisier himself? No worries if you're not. However, I'm certain you're acquainted with his fundamental principle: "Nothing is created, nothing is destroyed, everything is transformed." This principle beautifully encompasses the essence of this card: letting go of the past, whether it's a part of ourselves, a relationship, or a career path, is never an easy feat. It requires embracing change and growth, which can be both painful and necessary, particularly when they entail significant transformations. In relationships, it signifies a fresh beginning: if there was a previous crisis, we have acquired insights into what wasn't working and embark on a new chapter of the relationship, symbolizing that "things will be different from now on."

But declaring a new chapter is not always enough. When it comes to relationships, whether they're romantic, family-related, or friendships, being realistic is key. If there's a chance for growth, things can improve, but it's important to let go of what no longer serves us. So, today's lesson is out with the old, in with the new. You know what I mean, Bae, right? It's time to bring closure and move on to something better. So, don't hold on to lifeless situations. Ignored problems can only worsen. But just how lifeless is the relationship we're discussing? With this card, we begin a process of self-reflection, forgiveness, and new beginnings. Like wiping the slate clean and starting fresh. In our professional lives, this can be a turning point, an opportunity for a "system update" that empowers us (or, as always, our beloved querent—Ms. Betty) to become the best versions of ourselves. We undergo a transformation to manifest the changes we envisioned in the previous months.

Likewise, in this situation, crafting a well-thought-out resignation letter and waving a friendly goodbye can be the drastic yet necessary step to dive into brand new projects—for death need not be an absolute end, but rather a new beginning.

The cons of Death

When encountering this card during a reading with Ms. Betty, it is crucial to handle the situation discreetly. Why do I emphasize this? Well, this card indicates circumstances where the person seeking guidance has recognized a void in a specific area of their life or has endured a painful process of letting go. However, they face difficulties in fully accepting and moving forward. Often, the separation or break was not their choice, making it challenging for them to come to terms with it, thereby impeding their progress toward the future. Although the querent may deny any lingering attachment to the past, insisting that they have moved on, deep down, the truth reveals otherwise. They resist embracing the inevitable change. If the querent allows, it is essential to delve deeper into their circumstances and explore other aspects of their life where they can redirect their efforts, progressing toward a transformed and renewed self and refraining from clinging to what belongs to the past. What are they holding on to and why? These matters should be discussed with Ms. Betty.

Consider this analogy: Picture yourself postponing a seasonal wardrobe swap-out and finding yourself in August, sifting through heavy coats and jackets just to reach a t-shirt. Does that sound comfortable? More importantly, does it make sense? I understand that you may be thinking that comparing a relationship situation to a wardrobe swap is a stretch, and you're absolutely right, my dear Bae. However, it raises the question: how much space does this situation occupy in your life, preventing you from letting go of what is outdated or stagnant? Furthermore, how much do these dynamics hinder new growth, not only in the situation that needs to change but also in other aspects of your life? Take a moment to reflect on this point, embrace the seasonal change in your life, and open yourself up to the new opportunities that await. Despite its name, the Death card is a catalyst for action, brimming with life. Embrace that vitality within yourself!

Death's advice

"Grab the pruning shears and begin trimming, like shaping a bonsai tree to promote new growth. In this process, the act of trimming away the excess not only enhances the beauty of the plant but also allows for fresh shoots to flourish. And always remember, trimmed foliage becomes nourishing compost, fueling the growth of future plants."

A PLAYLIST FOR DEATH
Apply Some Pressure—Maxïmo Park
The Times They Are A-Changin'—Bob Dylan
Death Is Not the End—Nick Cave and the Bad Seeds
Everyboy's Changing—Keane

SONGS FROM ITALY
Insieme a Te Non ci Sto Più—Caterina Caselli
Ballo in Fa Diesis Minore—Angelo Branduardi

XIV

TEMPERANCE

XIV · TEMPERANCE · The ambiguous card

In a moment of tranquility, we encounter a familiar scene found in traditional Tarot decks: an angelic figure delicately pouring fluid from one vessel to another with utmost precision. This graceful act, like that of skilled bartenders, represents the residues left behind after facing the transformative power of the Death card. It's as if the angel is washing away what remains of our past selves, resembling a revitalizing cleanse.

Similar to a talented mixologist, the art lies in balancing the elements harmoniously, without one overpowering the others. This process demands both care and precision. The best outcomes take time. This card honors patience and gentleness. I can imagine you, dear Bae, anxiously tapping your nails at the very idea of "patience" following the wise teachings of the Hanged Man card. However, in this instance, waiting represents the steady and gradual flow of events, like water meandering its way downstream. Slowly but surely it reaches its destination.

This is the essence of Temperance: to teach us how to allow things to unfold naturally and avoid becoming frustrated. It's a challenging concept, especially as I write this during the transit of Mars and Mercury. It also serves as a personal mantra for me, and I hope it can bring comfort to you as well. 😊

Where do we find Temperance in everyday life?

We discover the essence of Temperance within our friends, who radiate a soothing energy and bring us serenity through their words and gestures. It's like a finely balanced recipe, where every ingredient and flavor effortlessly blend together in perfect harmony. As one of the four cardinal virtues, you might have come across it if you've explored classical studies. Moreover, individuals working in the wellness sector, like holistic practitioners, can also be closely linked to this Arcanum.

Given that this card typically depicts an angel and represents the harmonious interplay of elements, I personally find a connection with the concept of gender fluidity.

Level of intensity of Temperance

The intensity of this Arcanum depends entirely on your (or Ms. Betty's) inner serenity and the ability to allow things to flow naturally. For some it might be easier, but if chaos and disorder tend to rule in your life, it is definitely harder. Hence, I give it a 5 out of 10, which is the middle ground.

The pros of Temperance

The Temperance card delves into the art of finding peace and balance amidst an increasingly fast-paced and productivity-driven world, pushing the limits of our physical and mental well-being. It reminds us to allow things to unfold at their own pace, without unnecessary pressure. This card speaks of the power of adaptation, compromise, contentment, and appreciation for the present moment (although if you prefer a more adventurous path, the Devil card might hold greater appeal—but beware, as it requires embracing the lessons that Temperance teaches us!). Creating harmony with our surroundings becomes essential, as well as choosing companions who align with our chosen lifestyle. In matters of the heart, it offers a sense of comfort, but some may perceive it as a lack of excitement.

While beneficial, this card represents a positive yet somewhat lacking aspect in relationships. It suggests mutual support and kindness between partners but may lack passion and physical intimacy. This doesn't necessarily imply a problem, so it's wise to explore this aspect further with discretion. Temperance also highlights the value of friendship. However, be cautious if this card appears in a spread where Ms. Betty inquires about the potential for romance with someone she knows and likes. In the absence of additional cards signifying romantic or physical involvement, there is a potential for finding ourselves in the "friend zone." It's important to note, however, that if cards such as the Emperor, Devil, or Sun appear, it can indicate the potential for a friends-with-benefits arrangement. When it comes to work-related inquiries, the workplace fosters a positive environment, no drama, and an overall tranquil atmosphere. The key advice is to approach tasks in a composed and precise manner, meticulously assessing the factors that work in our favor and exploring ways to integrate them effectively for the desired outcomes. As the saying goes, "still waters run deep," a concept exemplified by the Strength card we've previously encountered—a valuable reminder of its significance. It's crucial to avoid putting unnecessary pressure on ourselves and not to panic at the first obstacle. Our goals can be achieved through patience and resilience.

The cons of Temperance

This card reminds me of Vasco Rossi, the Italian rock singer, and a verse in one of his songs, "I want to live a reckless life." When Temperance is unfavorable, we are following this verse to the letter.

Our energy scatters in all directions, our lives descend into disarray, while we stumble through a cluttered home, surrounded by junk food boxes and scattered clothing, desperately trying to recall where we misplaced our keys—or perhaps our sanity. The disorder that permeates our existence goes beyond mere disorganization; it seeps into our emotions and relationships. If we are not the root cause of this turmoil, then we must try to identify what is causing it. The rushed pressure of someone or something can cause us to become lost in all the chaos and sacrifice the peace we should be striving for. In order to handle the situation in the best way, it's essential to step back and look at it objectively, analyzing what is causing us such stress and finding ways to regain some balance. Everybody's needs are different in these kinds of circumstances, so finding a relevant and effective way to bring yourself back to calm should be tailored to suit your own personal needs as well as recognizing the importance of the current situation. I believe it's crucial for us to address this, particularly in today's context, where the New Age movement inundates us with advice on toxic positivity—encouraging constant happiness and positivity while disregarding any feelings of sadness or distress. What we should truly strive for is genuine well-being, acknowledging our present circumstances and embracing our individuality, allowing us to truly listen to ourselves and disregard any external pressures that push us to perform at our best in the blink of an eye. When it comes to matters of the heart, it's important to approach them with a sense of tranquility and a clear mindset. It's not about rushing into decisions, but rather calmly reflecting and calming any feeling of anxiety. Is Ms. Betty looking for a relationship right now? It could be that the timing isn't right just yet, and it might be wise for her to prioritize her well-being and personal development before pursuing it. When it comes to work, it's natural to not be as productive as usual, and it's important to be understanding of this rather than pressuring ourselves. Change will come eventually, but it may not be immediate, so going with the flow—just like a river does—is the best approach. What's the atmosphere like in the workplace? Is it stressful and competitive? Are we pushing ourselves beyond our limits? It's important to maintain a balanced approach and prioritize our health. Don't forget to stay hydrated and drink plenty of water!

Temperance's advice

"Accepting present circumstances for what they are doesn't mean giving up; rather, it entails finding ways to achieve your goals with minimal exertion. In fact, there are instances when inaction requires the greatest effort of all."

A PLAYLIST FOR TEMPERANCE
Venus as a Boy—Björk
No Pressure—Justin Bieber
Get the Balance Right—Depeche Mode
Go with the Flow—Queens of the Stone Age
Ebony and Ivory—Paul McCartney and Stevie Wonder

SONGS FROM ITALY
Finché la Barca Va—Orietta Berti

XV · THE DEVIL ·
The cool one

Together with Death, which I mentioned a few pages ago, and the Tower, which we'll discuss shortly, Arcanum XV holds a rather infamous reputation. They form the trio of the spooky cards, sending shivers down the poor querents' spine whenever I unveil one of them during a reading. I can't help but notice the startled reaction it elicits, as Ms. Betty nervously crosses herself and thinks an exorcist is needed. The figure of the Devil, present in various religions under different names, is rarely depicted as benevolent or someone you'd want to have a coffee with. In the Western world, the negative connotations stem from the prevalence of Catholicism. However, in the pagan world, such figures were not feared, and the worship of gods like Pan or Cernunnos, revered by pre-Christian groups, became ammunition for the Inquisition, who likely saw them as representations of the Demon. Pan, often depicted as a satyr with a prominent phallus, is closely associated with themes of masturbation and non-procreative sex, qualities traditionally linked to the Devil Arcanum. Let's not overlook the tale of Lucifer, once God's favored angel, who ultimately fell from grace. Some religions equate him with Satan, despite the fact that his name actually means "bearer of light," an ironic contradiction when considering the Devil's image. However, we're pragmatic individuals, aren't we, Bae? It's in this pragmatic approach that we must confront this Arcanum, which doesn't necessarily signify pure evil, or at least not directly. Rather, it delves into themes that can be quite enjoyable when approached with the right mindset—money, sex, the pleasures of life, and ambition.

Where do we find the Devil in everyday life?

The Devil embodies a magnetic presence that is hard to resist, almost addictive in nature. This card represents indulgence in all aspects of life (and hopefully, my dear Bae, you embody that spirit, too!). It encompasses themes of money and sexuality, highlighting the allure of wealth and pleasure. In some interpretations, it also delves into the realm of domination, evoking associations with BDSM and the roles of masters and mistresses. This card speaks to those who hold a strong attachment to material possessions, seeking stability and luxury through ambitious pursuits. However, it's important to note the negative aspects as well. The Devil serves as a tempter, leading us astray from discipline and luring us into toxic relationships or destructive habits. It represents emotional dependencies, be it various addictions, drugs, or toxic relationships which repeatedly cause us harm.

> **Lucy93**
> Hello, Redie. I recently conducted a Tarot reading regarding an upcoming job interview, and the Devil card appeared upright. This has left me feeling anxious and unsure. I'm not sure if this indicates potential career advancements or if it suggests that the person conducting the interview might have ill intentions. It has made me quite hesitant and apprehensive about attending the interview.

> **SoloRedie**
> Let me reassure you—The presence of the Devil card indicates a strong influence of material energies, particularly in relation to finances. It suggests that the job you are interviewing for has the potential to be highly lucrative, but it will require dedicated effort on your part. If you can demonstrate your determination and focus during the interview, you are likely to receive a favorable outcome that aligns with your expectations, if not exceed them. As for the interviewer, there is no indication of malice or inappropriate behavior. Perhaps hope that it won't be Mr. Grey from Fifty Shades of Grey. Unless, of course, you don't mind that!

Level of intensity of the Devil

When the Devil card appears upright, the challenge of managing its energy can be rated at a 3 out of 10. Giving in to our impulses and surrendering to passion can bring a sense of liberation and delight. However, when reversed, things get a bit more tricky. We are confronted with the need to break free from the chains that bind us, and this process can be exceptionally complex. I would rate the intensity at an 8 out of 10!

The pros of the Devil

Seductive, determined, adventurous, driven by desires, and brimming with vitality. I'm not referring to myself, but rather to the Devil Arcanum. It's time to embrace the positive aspects of this card and let go of the negative connotations. When it appears, we're encouraged to let go of our inhibitions, indulge in pleasure, and embark on thrilling adventures. If you've been responsible with your resources, go ahead and treat yourself to a shopping spree. If a one-night stand is what you're craving, now is the perfect opportunity. The key is to keep it casual, drama-free, and no strings attached. The Devil primarily influences the physical realm rather than the spiritual, making it easier to avoid becoming emotionally entangled. However, it's often mistakenly believed that this card doesn't apply to stable relationships, when in fact it can be quite the opposite.

This could be a perfect opportunity for a couple to reignite the flame that has faded away due to the routine of daily life. They can spice up their sex life by exploring and experimenting with new things, or even take their commitment to the next level by considering a real estate investment. Why am I providing such specific details? It's because the Devil's influence extends to the material domain—the tangible aspects of our existence—and what could be more concrete and substantial than buying a property?

Addressing the subject of betrayal, if Ms. Betty suspects infidelity in the relationship, the presence of the Devil card affirms that there is indeed betrayal occurring. What's intriguing is that this betrayal goes beyond mere emotional betrayal and indicates physical betrayal as well. It's important to note that it's generally advised to refrain from investigating others. However, ultimately, you should trust your instincts and make decisions based on what feels right in that particular situation. Speaking of being practical and concrete, this Arcanum offers guidance to transform abstract ideas into tangible projects. In a nutshell, this card is highly pragmatic and focused on the real world. In the realm of work, it indicates concrete opportunities and lucrative contracts. With the Devil card, as I mentioned earlier, we also delve into themes of wealth, possessions, and investments, including real estate, which hold significant potential. Broadly speaking, this card grants us the ability to assert dominance and maintain control over the various situations in which it appears.

The cons of the Devil

When the Devil card is reversed, I often describe it as "a fun game that's gotten out of hand." While indulging in superficial pleasure can bring some benefits, the drawbacks arise when these take hold of us, making it difficult to break free, and become deeply ingrained in our lives. However, this card provides the querent with an opportunity to reflect on why they are unable to escape these toxic patterns that poison their life and exert control over them. It's not limited to substances like alcohol and drugs or sex and gambling. In terms of relationships, the querent may develop a dependency on individuals who are likely to be narcissists or manipulators, continuously allowing them back into their life as if nothing happened. They find themselves chained to their ups and downs, perhaps because they feel powerless to change the situation or they believe that it will eventually get better. Another aspect to consider is the tendency to fall into repetitive behavioral patterns, which unconsciously cause us to make the same mistakes over and over again, in a never-ending loop. In work, we often find ourselves enslaved by a situation that may offer financial rewards but ultimately limits our growth and prevents us from breaking free. The unfavorable presence of the Devil card brings an oppressive energy, prompting us to contemplate how we can break these chains and regain control. A crucial piece of advice for freedom is learning to assert ourselves by saying no and reclaiming our independence.

The Devil's advice

"Would you like to embrace a fulfilling life? Are you eager to experience a sense of well-being and transform your dreams into reality? It's time to roll up your sleeves and put in the work, my friend! Stay rooted in reality as you strive for personal growth and be courageous enough to challenge both the world around you and your own limitations."

A PLAYLIST FOR THE DEVIL
Work Bitch—Britney Spears
Material Girl—Madonna
Sympathy for the Devil—The Rolling Stones
S&M—Rihanna
Rehab—Amy Winehouse
El Diablo—YEИDRY

THE TOWER

XVI · Hit me Baby one more time · THE TOWER

To help you understand how this Arcanum operates, let me share the thought process behind writing the chapter on the Magician. As I contemplated the title, I had a sudden and unexpected light bulb moment related to the Tower card. The perfect alignment with the Britney Spears song "Hit Me Baby One More Time" for Arcanum XVI became evident. Did I ignore this distraction? No. Did I anticipate this? Not at all. Initially, my intention was to focus on the Magician, but I chose not to dismiss the idea; instead, I recognized the need for the Tower to be considered at that precise moment and wholeheartedly embraced this unexpected inspiration.

Now let me dive into the origins of this card. Do you remember the captivating tale of the Tower of Babel? Allow me to share it with you. In essence, a group of individuals believed they had conceived an ingenious plan: they set out to construct a tower that would reach the heavens, envisioning a place where humanity could live together without the need to populate other lands. During that time, they shared a common language, which greatly facilitated their progress. However, God noticed their undertaking and decided to intervene. Chaos ensued as He caused the workers to speak different languages, leading to a breakdown in communication and an abrupt halt to the ambitious construction that aimed to touch the sky. It truly is fascinating, isn't it?

Next, let's delve into the moral of this tale. Ambition unaccompanied by personal growth and a reluctance to step outside our comfort zone (symbolized by speaking the same language and avoiding the pursuit of new challenges) are formidable adversaries to the Tower.

Where do we find the Tower in everyday life?

The Tower card can symbolize all that is sudden and abrupt: an explosion, a lightning strike, an impromptu protest, or even flash mobs (if they still exist, considering they were quite popular about a decade ago). It also represents unannounced natural disasters like floods, earthquakes, and hurricanes, all of which possess immense destructive power. If we think of the Tower in terms of people, it represents those who are incredibly scatty and messy, leaving all their belongings—clothes, documents, and so on—scattered all over the place wherever they go. It also includes those individuals who—once they enter our lives—manage to completely turn it upside down like a whirlwind has just blown through—leaving us completely baffled and bewildered.

Crash
I read that, when the Tower appears upside down, it means that in a given situation or problem we have run out of solutions and there is nothing more we can do. Is this true?

SoloRedie
I believe that every problem has a solution, even though it may require hard work. Starting from scratch, with a clean slate, can be challenging, but it also presents numerous opportunities. It's important not to see the results of the reading as an absolute verdict. Instead, let's view the Tower card as a reminder to take action and approach our problems with a broader perspective. We shouldn't let ourselves be defined by our problems, but rather see them as an incentive to explore new possibilities.

Level of intensity of the Tower

This Arcanum truly embodies a captivating intensity, scoring a perfect 10 out of 10. Whether it appears upright or reversed, it signals the need for us to roll up our sleeves, clear away the clutter, and reorganize the pieces. However, this time around, we must begin from the bottom rather than the top.

The pros of the Tower

The Tower is widely regarded as one of the most feared cards in the Major Arcana. It symbolizes destruction and downfall, and witnessing the collapse of our carefully constructed plans is never a pleasant experience. This concept can be challenging to accept, particularly because when the Tower appears, it is often sudden and violent. However, let's pause and reconsider. Could it be that the Tower actually exposes the weaknesses in our relationships or situations that were built on unstable foundations? Perhaps we continued to build upon these shaky grounds, deliberately turning a blind eye to the impending tragedy. We pushed ourselves too far, and then… BOOM! The wake-up call slaps us right in the face. Yet, amidst the wreckage, there lies a precious opportunity for redemption. We have the chance to rebuild, but this time with stronger foundations, having gleaned invaluable lessons from our past failures. It presents an invitation for change, an ultimatum urging us to embrace flexibility and let go of resistance. Moving forward from this turning point, our sole path is that of relentless improvement, armed with a deep understanding of the circumstances that led to our downfall.

When it comes to love, the Tower card can symbolize the classic tale of love at first sight—a sudden and unexpected meeting that takes us by surprise when we aren't actively seeking romance. It has the ability to emerge in places or contexts that we never imagined could lead to intriguing and meaningful connections.

If a relationship is in progress, something unexpected can dramatically alter its course, like some surprising news or an impulsive decision. The outcome depends on the health of the bond: if it's strong, it may disrupt the routine but ultimately strengthen it. If it's weak, it's unlikely to survive the blow, allowing us to embrace the freedom we've regained. In work, our resignation or even a long-awaited layoff will provide a much-needed opportunity to break free from a situation that has accumulated excessive stress and strain. In such cases, the rupture becomes an inevitable and necessary step toward a brighter future.

The cons of the Tower

Picture a desolate wasteland in the aftermath of a hurricane, with debris scattered and nothingness all around. Those who had prepared for this event may have secured their windows or salvaged what they could. However, for those who were partly aware but failed to take action, recovering from this devastating phenomenon becomes a daunting task. The reversed Tower card mirrors this scenario. It arrives unexpectedly, yet if we revisit the notion I mentioned earlier, where unstable foundations crumble, we might have sensed that something was amiss, yet chose to ignore it. And now, we find ourselves with nothing, attempting to gather the fragments of what once stood. This reluctance to acknowledge the deteriorating situation perpetuates our struggle to rise from the ruins. Consequently, the reversed Tower card signifies a rupture. In relationships, it manifests as inevitable conflicts that abruptly sever the bond, leaving us with limited lessons learned and a lack of clarity to move forward without that person. The Tower card can also signify a partial rupture within a bond, profoundly impacting the individuals involved in the relationship. Additionally, it has the power to expose the hidden dynamics that we often choose to ignore, shedding light on the cracks in relationships that are already worn out or burdened by monotony.

In work, the risk of burnout looms, leading to panic attacks, sudden bursts of anger, and uncontrolled reactions. Unexpected job termination can throw us into a state of despair. Even if we believed we were adequately prepared for an exam or interview, our ambition, if not supported by proper preparation or experience, will inevitably face the consequences. This card serves as a reminder not to overestimate our abilities. It is crucial for Ms. Betty to reflect on the importance of understanding that if something didn't work out and no efforts were made to improve it, it becomes an opportunity to learn rather than grieve. She must recognize that, despite the intense stress she may be experiencing, these situations should be viewed as chances for growth, rather than as a punishment. The Tower also brings a sense of liberation, and that's why we need to remind Ms. Betty of the possibility of rising above her circumstances and rewriting her own story. She must realize that as much as she may have been tied to that situation resembling a two-legged stool unable to stand for much longer, she cannot continue living in such a way.

The Tower's advice

"Have you heard the saying 'When one door closes, another one opens'? That's exactly what I embody. I possess the power to forcefully close doors behind me and open new ones with tremendous strength. While my actions may initially create chaos, they ultimately bring about order by offering you a chance for a new beginning. So instead of dwelling on the past, let's embrace this opportunity and make the most of it. Don't waste time crying over spilled milk; let's seize the moment!"

A PLAYLIST FOR THE TOWER
Seek & Destroy—Metallica
Destroy Everything You Touch—Ladytron
Wrecking Ball—Miley Cyrus
Earthquake—DJ Fresh vs. Diplo feat. Dominique Young Unique

SONGS FROM ITALY
La Torre di Babele—Edoardo Bennato
Hanno Ucciso l'Uomo Ragno—883

THE STAR

XVII · Children of
THE STARS

After the upheaval depicted by the Tower card, we find ourselves in a serene landscape, markedly distinct from the arduous journey we've navigated since the Hanged Man card. It's as if we are slowly ascending from our own version of Dante's Inferno, which began with Arcanum XII. Speaking of Dante, he concludes the final verse of the Inferno with the word "stars," the same word that concludes Purgatory and Heaven ("Pure and disposed to mount unto the stars" and "the love that moves the sun and all the stars"). With the Star Arcanum, we delve into the concept of innocent desire and explore the etymology of the verb "desire" itself. Desire is what we feel when we see shooting stars, evoking both a sense of longing for the loss or absence of something delightful, similar to the stars themselves, and the hopeful anticipation of witnessing another one. The essence of this card also revolves around hope and the ambition to create something positive that will bring us comfort in the future.

Where do we find the Star in everyday life?

When we view the world through rose-tinted spectacles, embracing an optimistic perspective, we embody the essence of the Star card. In our everyday lives, we encounter this Arcanum when we let go of fear and uncertainty about the future. The popular saying "que sera, sera" or "what will be, will be" resonates deeply with the essence of this card. Those who possess a lighthearted and playful nature, who choose not to dwell excessively on life's dramas, become the true advocates of the stars. Conversely, when the Star card appears in an inverted position, it represents individuals who consistently feel underappreciated or hold a cynical view, expecting the worst in every situation. If you have a green thumb, have a profound interest in astrology, or eagerly study celestial phenomena, then the Star card aligns perfectly with your journey.

Level of intensity of the Star

On a scale of 1 to 10, the intensity level of this Arcanum is about 4. It doesn't rely solely on concrete facts but rather on our state of mind. It operates on an emotional level and can fluctuate significantly, whether it appears upright or reversed. Even the tiniest thing can plunge us into despair, yet an equally small joy has the power to incredibly uplift our spirits. As this state is transient, its unfavorable aspect doesn't weigh heavily enough to completely overshadow it.

The pros of the Star

Roman slang is renowned for its humor and sarcasm, reflecting the easygoing and playful nature of the locals. In Rome, there's a saying I adore, which translates as "What are you laughing at, is it your party?" It's playfully said to someone who is jolly without any apparent reason. This saying always comes to mind when I think of Arcanum XVII because this card, when interpreted positively, symbolizes the ability to be happy without a specific reason, embracing joy and a carefree spirit as inherent traits, rather than being dependent on external factors. It radiates an aura of optimism and unwavering faith in the future, even in a world that may appear less than promising, where the ability to dream is becoming increasingly scarce. When this card appears in a reading, it infuses the atmosphere with a sense of fun, be it in a professional, personal, or emotional context. This surge of optimism encourages us to imagine and pursue upcoming projects, while our positive mindset brings us closer to realizing our dreams.

Similar to what we experience with Temperance, the environment in which we find ourselves is supportive and friendly, making it easier to maintain a positive and cheerful outlook as we progress toward our dreams. This uplifting atmosphere extends to relationships, whether they are new or ongoing. When it comes to upcoming projects or the possibility of conceiving, the presence of the Star is a positive indication, particularly if it aligns with the Empress, the World, or Temperance. Should Ms. Betty's question be work related, this card brings favorable energy. The work environment is comforting, and colleagues may become more than just coworkers, with potential for meaningful relationships outside of work. Moreover, success and self-realization feel like achievable endeavors.

The cons of the Star

When this card is reversed, the dominant feeling it evokes is that we tend to react negatively to things. I can't think of any better way to describe the emotion associated with this card. As I mentioned earlier, the stars operate in a realm that is connected to our emotions rather than being focused on concrete aspects. In its reversed position, the card amplifies feelings of anxiety and melancholy, stemming from negative thoughts rather than realistic worries or actual events. This reversed card indicates that our tendency toward negativity is intertwined with our approach to life. If we are accustomed to experiencing anxiety about the future even before it unfolds or if we become depressed after facing setbacks, we struggle to envision and plan ahead. In such cases, the future itself is perceived as a threat, making it challenging for us to dream and set goals. This card can also indicate an inclination to indulge in self-pity, not necessarily due to a valid reason, but rather stemming from an inherent pessimistic attitude and tendency to complain. The advice here is to confront this mindset head-on and make an effort to stimulate a more proactive response. While the context in which this Arcanum appears is likely not all pleasant and positive, succumbing to personal melancholy can have far-reaching consequences, potentially seeping into areas of life that are actually going relatively well. This emotional state has a ripple effect, triggering a downward spiral of sadness and an overwhelming feeling of hopelessness. The stars, with their ever-shifting nature, possess the power to swiftly transform a moment of bad mood into a good one, as soon as something favorable occurs. I deliberately did not specify their influence across the different aspects I typically analyze (personal, social, work-related) because it impacts them all in a similar manner. It engenders a sense of nihilism that restricts our vision to the present moment, making us feel as if tomorrow holds no promise of anything new. It perfectly echoes the sentiment expressed in the punk slogan of 1977: "No Future."

The Star's advice

"While it is true that I resonate with the realm of the soul, please do not underestimate my significance as a card. In fact, it is from this very essence that the energy emanates, guiding us to fulfill our true potential. I like to think of each star as a liberated soul, freed from the confines of the earthly plane, ascending to the heavens, and radiating alongside its celestial companions. Perhaps my imagination ventures into exaggeration but allow me to dream—for dreaming causes no harm."

A PLAYLIST FOR THE STAR
Hope Is a Dangerous Thing for a Woman Like Me to Have—Lana Del Rey
Medley: Aquarius/Let the Sunshine In (The Flesh Failures)—The 5th Dimension
You've Got a Friend in Me—Randy Newman
Barbie Girl—Aqua

SONGS FROM ITALY
Futura—Lucio Dalla
Figli Delle Stelle—Alan Sorrentiù

XVIII · What a MOON!

Since ancient times, the Moon has occupied a prominent place in poetry, literature, and music, casting its celestial influence upon human life. It plays a subtle yet profoundly significant role in our existence. For centuries, people have relied on its guidance to synchronize with the rhythms of cultivation, tides, fertility, and even haircuts (I'm sure you have at least once waited on a waxing moon to trim your hair). Its assistance and influence bring about changes that may often go unnoticed but can be seen as the aftermath of the monumental upheaval depicted by the Tower Arcanum.

The Moon assumes a remarkable role as the card of "aftershocks," unmasking the concealed depths of our very core, bringing them into the light. Within the Major Arcana, the Moon functions as an archaeologist, adeptly unearthing the dormant aspects that have been concealed and overlooked, compelling us to give them our undivided attention and resolve them once and for all. Symbolizing the essence of the Dark Lady, it extends an invitation to bravely confront and explore the profound depths of our own shadow self.

Where do we find the Moon in everyday life?

When I contemplate this card, two iconic figures from popular culture immediately spring to mind: Lana Del Rey, effortlessly personifying this Arcanum with her retro aesthetic and melancholic melodies, and Sailor Moon, for reasons that should be crystal clear! (Bonus points if you remember!) Furthermore, I envision all those who possess an enchanting, enigmatic allure, radiating a mysterious charm that thrives in the depths of darkness. These often so-called "cursed artists," like Arthur Rimbaud, Jim Morrison, and Amy Winehouse, are captivated by the past and seek solace in the echoes of bygone eras, as if they were misplaced in time. They are the dreamers with eyes wide open, blessed with prophetic visions and an innate maternal instinct that extends far beyond their own offspring. Moreover, I associate this card with professions intertwined with secrecy and the subconscious, such as private investigation, psychology, and the mystical arts of fortune telling.

Level of intensity of the Moon

The depth and intricacy of the work associated with this card are truly remarkable, earning it a solid 10 out of 10 for complexity. It requires a profound sense of centeredness, where one must allow their emotions to flow freely and embrace the full intensity of their instincts, all while avoiding becoming overwhelmed.

The pros of the Moon

While it may not come naturally to Ms. Betty, the presence of this card indicates the importance of nurturing a deep connection with our subconscious mind and emotions, allowing them to flow freely. It is essential to trust our instincts, embracing our sixth sense and imagination, and letting go of strict rational control. It's worth clarifying the distinction between the Moon and the High Priestess. The High Priestess uses reason to interpret intuitive insights, symbolized by the crescent moon as their receptive antenna, filtering signals from higher realms. The Moon, on the other hand, represents pure intuition—an expansive ocean we must learn to navigate. Under this celestial influence, situations take on a gentle, calm quality. Emotionally, we may experience intense connections that are still in the process of solidifying. If the connections are already established, we may find ourselves in a nearly telepathic bond, where a single glance conveys immediate understanding, or we can perceive the needs of others even from a distance. Emotions play a vital role in relationships, even when we are single. It's important to understand our feelings when we are in our own company, addressing unresolved issues from the past and gradually illuminating our path toward self-discovery. This self-awareness sets the foundation for sharing our authentic selves with others in the future. In a professional context, this card signifies the presence of intuitive insights that can guide us on our journey. How does this feeling resonate with you? Does it propel you toward a particular choice or steer you away from it? Consider asking Ms. Betty about her recent professional experiences or, if she doesn't have a profession, what direction her intuition is pointing her toward.

The Moon also speaks to creativity. Unlike the Magician, which sparks new ventures, or the Empress, which embodies aesthetic beauty and pleasure, the Moon taps into an emotional realm of creativity. It encourages us to channel our innermost selves into our endeavors.

The cons of the Moon

When in an unfavorable position, the Moon card can present itself as perplexing and inscrutable. Its depiction is often portrayed as a soft silver glow that gracefully dances upon the calm surface of the water. This imagery symbolizes a reflective surface that conceals its hidden depths. If that ethereal light were to fade away, the bottom would become obscured, transforming the once serene, glowing water into murky and daunting depths.

If you don't have a traditional deck, you can draw parallels to the famous Dark Side of the Moon—the concealed aspect that remains unseen.

These two sides represent different facets of the same entity: one is clear, visible, and known, while the other is mysterious, unsettling, and deceptive. The latter represents our accumulated fears, unnamed and buried emotions, or what I like to call "dust under the carpet." How much confusion arises from not questioning ourselves or openly expressing our thoughts? How many lies do we tell, especially to ourselves, out of fear of direct confrontation or confronting emotionally uncomfortable situations? When this card appears, the answer is: too many. When we avoid seeking clarification, the lack of confirmation from the listener can give rise to feelings of uncertainty, which in turn can fuel paranoia or lead to delusional thinking.

This map of the mind reveals two significant cards from the Major Arcana that, when coupled with the Moon (especially when reversed), warrant careful consideration. I'm referring to the Magician, whose presence amplifies their ability to manipulate and shape reality through persuasive words, and the Fool, whose conjunction with the Moon creates a complex tapestry of distorted intuitions, ambiguous thoughts, and a profound detachment from reality. In such instances, my advice for Ms. Betty is to embark on a thorough exploration of these illusions and reestablish a solid grounding by focusing on verifiable truths.

Regarding emotions, when the Moon appears in a negative light, the lingering impact of past traumatic relationships can permeate present connections. It's crucial not to project the faults and mistakes of our past relationships onto our current partners. Instead, let us address any unresolved wounds we feel we've endured and foster emotional openness with our current partner, creating an environment of trust and transparency. Otherwise, we risk projecting feelings of resentment onto those who are currently by our side.

Secrets and betrayals carry a heavy weight on our conscience and must be addressed to preserve the integrity of our current relationships. This holds true even when we are alone: how can we forge new bonds if we still carry the pain of the past? If we want to really move forward, it is crucial to confront our past, heal from it and find closure.

In work, I strongly urge caution regarding what remains unsaid but can be sensed. When tensions arise, it is essential to identify their root cause. Could someone be plotting against us? Is our work ethic completely transparent?

It is important to consider the quality of our sleep, especially if Ms. Betty's inquiry revolves around personal growth or improving her lifestyle. The adverse influence of the Moon may result in insomnia and unsettling dreams. I suggest delving into the root causes and making rest a priority. The night holds valuable insights and guidance—it would be a shame not to embrace its wisdom.

The Moon's advice

"Trust the path I'm leading you on, my dear Bae. Even if it takes you into the depths of darkness, learn to navigate it, relying on your inner compass to guide you. Embrace the concept of darkness as a companion you can live with. Remember, the Bogeyman is only in stories!"

A PLAYLIST FOR THE MOON
Blue Velvet—Bobby Vinton
Moonlight Serenade—Glenn Miller
Claire de Lune—Claude Debussy
Dark Paradise—Lana Del Rey

SONGS FROM ITALY
Luna—Gianni Togni
L'Ombra della Luce—Franco Battiato

THE SUN

XIX · La vida es chula · THE SUN

After this journey through the darkness, starting with the Hanged Man and ending with the Moon, we find ourselves returning to the light. The Sun rises as it does each day, and all we can do is embrace its warmth as if we were sitting on the terrace of the *Café del Mar* in Ibiza. We have experienced various aspects of the soul, put in hard work, gotten our hands dirty, and walked hand in hand with our Dark Side. And now we bask under the benevolent gaze of this radiant star, which instills in us a desire to connect with others. We're filled with energy, the excitement is soaring, and our enthusiasm matches that of a lively summer beach party. Living under the Sun brings us joy because we have encountered and conquered the darkness.

Where do we find the Sun in everyday life?

This card is a vibrant embodiment of individuals who exude boundless enthusiasm, perpetually radiating a sunny energy that lights up any room. Their infectious smiles and unwavering zest for life make them natural magnets for group activities. The Sun card perfectly captures the essence of a jovial resort entertainer—a vivacious character who thrives on orchestrating lively group dances and orchestrating memorable events. It symbolizes those who are effortlessly surrounded by a close-knit circle of friends, those who have chosen to bask in the warmth of tropical locales where the sun is always shining, and those who embrace the ethos of Desigual's captivating slogan, "La Vida es Chula" (Life is Cool). Conversely, when positioned unfavorably, it evokes the image of individuals who dread being added to WhatsApp groups or harbor an aversion to collaborative teamwork.

Level of intensity of the Sun

Collaboration, sincerity, fun, warmth... the Sun can be quite intense to handle, especially if you're an introvert (or a Hermit) at heart! Nevertheless, it poses no significant challenge to overcome even when it is less favorable. So, let's give it a difficulty rating of 2 out of 10!

The pros of the Sun

When this card appears, it signifies a situation infused with immense strength and boundless enthusiasm to face those situations we no longer wish to keep to ourselves. We feel a desire to work together with others, rather than alone, with the aim of achieving a common goal. The longing to share this joy becomes our driving force. It urges Ms. Betty to connect with like-minded individuals who possess the same spirit, radiating passion toward this project that is destined to achieve resounding success. As we embark on this journey together, the burdens will feel lighter, and the experience of happiness shared will be immensely fulfilling. This Arcanum embodies a profound sincerity and a soul that shines with transparency, giving us a beautiful radiant aura. The era of deceit and intrigue has reached its end, paving the way for the benevolent light to guide our actions. We wholeheartedly embrace the present moment, cultivating a mindset firmly rooted in the here and now, avoiding unnecessary anxieties that stem from projecting ourselves into an unknown future.

This Arcanum adds a certain heat to the intimate sphere, much like Strength (which embodies physical vitality) and the Devil (known for its irresistible passion). Both in new and in long-term relationships, this can translate into a playful and enjoyable physical bond where both partners feel at ease and fully embrace their intimacy. In a more established relationship, it signifies working together as a team to pursue shared life goals, whether that means finding happiness and serenity or navigating challenges while remaining solid and caring for each other. Honesty becomes the cornerstone of such a relationship, where truth is the key to making things thrive.

In a workplace setting, this card signifies a lively and celebratory atmosphere, where team-building efforts have been successful, and individuals are not engaged in unhealthy competition against one another. It represents a sense of sisterhood and brotherhood that unites people and encourages seeking out collaborators who share the same joyful spirit. It is an incredibly motivating Arcanum! However, we must exercise caution and avoid exposing all this light and positivity to the wrong people. There is a risk of attracting what we call "energetic vampires," individuals who drain the vital energy from others, leaving us feeling depleted.

The advice is to steer Ms. Betty toward partnering with collaborators who are on the same wavelength as this will ensure a harmonious and supportive working environment.

The cons of the Sun

Let's start with the understanding that the Sun card, much like the World card, is incredibly positive, to the extent that even in an unfavorable position, it does not signify anything irreparable. Its radiant light may dim, like a slightly wilting sunflower, indicating a certain coldness in our interactions and in our general approach to life. Relationships are characterized by formality, and displays of affection are infrequent, lacking warmth, and often limited to obligatory gestures. We find ourselves keeping a certain distance, and it's essential to discern whether this stems from a sense of pride or a broader detachment from social connections. Collaboration and forging meaningful partnerships hold little interest for us as we tend to conserve our vital energies exclusively for ourselves, avoiding group involvements and affiliations to sidestep potential clashes of ideas. This creates a gloomy state of mind, where even when there is sunshine all around us, we carry an inner negativity that dampens our overall enthusiasm. It is crucial to understand the underlying causes of this—whether it arises from clashing energies around us or our own inclination to maintain a practical outlook while masking underlying anxieties about the future. Remember that life unfolds in the present moment. When we constantly dwell on events that haven't even occurred yet, it hampers our ability to fully enjoy the simple pleasures that come our way every day. To break free from this pattern, we need to embrace the warmth and positivity that surrounds us. At work, we might find ourselves lacking enthusiasm for what we do, but we soldier on by pretending it's all okay. We keep a certain distance from our team and the tasks at hand, putting in minimal effort. However, it's important to acknowledge that we can't always shine when we're alone. There are times when we must join forces with others who are willing to lend a helping hand.

The unfavorable aspect of this card highlights a particular challenge in expressing our desires, often influenced by underlying self-esteem issues. Let's acknowledge our positive qualities and embark on a journey to showcase them in their full splendor. By embracing our strengths and cultivating self-confidence, we can generate a renewed sense of enthusiasm and create a brighter path ahead.

The Sun's advice

"Get your finest shades on, grab your fave crew and go enjoy the rediscovered zest for life! Don't forget the sunscreen!"

A PLAYLIST FOR THE SUN
Walking on Sunshine—Katrina and the Waves
Ray of Light—Madonna
We Are Family—Sister Sledge
Ain't No Mountain High Enough—Tammi Terrell feat. Marvin Gaye

SONGS FROM ITALY
Riccione—Thegiornalisti
Caliente, Caliente—Raffaella Carrà

JUDGEMENT

XX · JUDGMENT is a dj

Hey, can you believe we're almost done with the Major Arcana? It's crazy to think that not long ago, you picked up this book without any idea of where it would take you! But worry not, we still have the Minor Arcana to delve into, so you're stuck with me for a little while longer.

Can you feel your awareness expanding? Do you feel more self-assured now that you've discovered how the Arcana can be found in everyday life and the world around you? You could even consider writing your own book! If you think about it, the journey you've taken so far is like the theme of an engaging play, with its intriguing characters, unexpected twists and turns, and soon, the epic finale. You're on the verge of becoming a truly esteemed Tarot interpretation expert, and the Judgment card is here to validate that. It serves as proof that you've weathered the ups and downs of life, embarked on personal quests, and navigated relationships, all while gaining profound knowledge. Now, you have the ability to communicate your wisdom with clarity and impact, perhaps even on a grand stage. The show is yours!

Where do we find Judgment in everyday life?

This card can be connected to various mentors, much like the Hierophant. However, while the Hierophant focuses on transmitting and enforcing rules, the Judgment card aims to disseminate knowledge. We can encounter this Arcanum in individuals who inspire others through their actions and set an example for their community. It can be seen at celebratory events that mark significant milestones requiring extensive preparation, such as weddings or graduations. It represents a performance on stage, a published book, or simply the expression, "It's about time!" Personally, this card always brings to mind a DJ at the console, guiding the crowd to dance with their hands in the air. It reminds me of the first parties and concerts after the pandemic lockdown, which symbolized the end of a dark and isolated period and, for many, signified a rebirth. On the other hand, when I envision this card in an unfavorable aspect, it is associated with the well-known "impostor syndrome" or the missing puzzle piece that prevents us from putting it up on display.

Level of intensity of Judgment

The Judgment card assumes that much of the groundwork has already been done, and as the final step toward liberation and rebirth, it should be a seemingly straightforward journey. However, considering its less favorable aspect and the challenge of setting ourselves free from the judgments of others, this combination of factors leads me to rate its difficulty level as a 7 out of 10.

The pros of Judgment

This is the Arcanum of good news, where messages are proclaimed loudly and clearly. Picture the angelic trumpeter in traditional decks, portraying the Angel of Judgment. Keep that image in mind, as it helps us understand how these messages are delivered: with grandeur and officiality. It reminds me of Alexandra Stan's "Mr. Saxobeat" (yes, I know a sax is not a trumpet, but let's not nitpick). This card signifies a pivotal moment to take a bold leap into our true potential, fearlessly exposing ourselves to both external judgment and self-criticism. With a calm and confident heart, bolstered by our wealth of experiences, we recognize our own worth, knowledge, and abilities. We become eager to share them with others, knowing that the people around us support and appreciate our value. This support further reinforces our self-assurance.

It's worth noting that this card, like Temperance or the Stars, also speaks to the importance of close friendships and family connections. So, when considering its significance in a reading, it's worth exploring if these relationships play a role in the situation at hand. In matters of romance, it may be a time for a significant step forward or a chance to finally see the light at the end of the tunnel after overcoming personal challenges, such as the end of a relationship or a difficult ordeal. Overall, the Judgment card encourages us to embrace our strengths, step into the spotlight, and boldly express ourselves without fear of judgment. It's a call to celebrate our growth and embrace new possibilities with confidence and optimism. The Judgment card signifies a significant personal journey of growth and self-reflection. It represents the culmination of our efforts and the opportunity to reap the rewards. It's about knowing ourselves better, appreciating the challenges we've overcome, and having the confidence to showcase our knowledge and abilities to others. If Ms. Betty asks a work-related question and the Judgment card appears, it brings long-awaited confirmations and positive feedback. It's a moment for her to feel proud of her hard work and accomplishments. Additionally, she may find herself in a position to guide others who are going through similar experiences, offering them valuable and unbiased advice. This is the perfect card to find in a question regarding an exam or a test. Moreover, the Judgment card represents the courage to make decisions that will bring us happiness and fulfillment. It encourages us to embrace our true selves and take the necessary steps toward personal growth and transformation. It's a reminder to seize the moment, to step into the unknown with confidence, and to embrace the power of change.

The cons of Judgment

Others' judgment often acts as a formidable barrier to achieving our dreams, leaving us entangled in a web of uncertainties that constantly teeter on the edge of "I wish I could, but I can't." My dear Bae, the question I now pose to you requires utmost honesty: is it truly other people's judgment that holds you back, or could it be that you are projecting your own self-judgment onto others, constructing a convenient alibi to sabotage your own progress and shield yourself from vulnerability?

You may be familiar with the notorious "impostor syndrome," a complex defense mechanism that often manifests when we engage in activities that matter a lot to us, particularly those involving public exposure and financial implications. In these instances, we can't help but feel like a fraud despite our efforts and achievements because we are unable to believe that our success is deserved or legitimate. Our struggle lies in recognizing our self-worth and granting it the deserved value. Additionally, we may harbor a nagging sense of inadequacy, fearing that we lack the qualifications or competence to openly present ourselves to the critical eyes of the world. The looming apprehension of being unmasked by someone seemingly more adept in our chosen field further fuels our self-doubt. All of this is triggered by a strong insecurity and the fear of not living up to what others expect. We have a deep desire to succeed, but it feels out of reach because we hesitate to take the leap, even though we've come a long way. The challenge with this card is that the risk of self-doubt is just around the corner. We struggle with other people's success and find it difficult to step into the spotlight and claim our own rightful place. So, step out into the open and stop constantly judging yourself as if you were your own worst enemy. Give yourself the space and opportunity to shine on stage and grab the microphone (or the trumpet). We all have our insecurities—me, you, Ms. Betty. And despite the fact that there will always be people who know more than us—and this applies to everybody—doesn't mean we have to hide. In general, when this card is unfavorable, the attitude is often quite passive. We see a Ms. Betty who waits for others to make the first move or for negative situations to solve themselves. For example, in matters of love, she expects her partner to leave the relationship or hopes for a reconciliation if the relationship has ended. If she's single, she may be waiting for love to come knocking at her door. However, there was a mural near where I grew up that said, "Wake up, life doesn't wait for you," and that's exactly the advice I would give when this unfavorable card appears. In the workplace, we may desire more responsibility, but we struggle to prove that we deserve it. We may feel inadequate or that our voices aren't being heard enough. But it's important to remember that we have the potential to grow and assert ourselves.

Judgment's advice

"What have you taken away from your experiences, Bae? Declare it from a high place, a podium, a balcony or even shout it out from a car window. Your wisdom could help others, so don't pass up the opportunity to spread the word!"

A PLAYLIST FOR JUDGMENT

I Will Survive—Gloria Gaynor

Alive and Kicking—Simple Minds

California—Grimes

Mr. Saxobeat—Alexandra Stan

I'm Coming Out—Diana Ross

After the Storm—Kali Uchis feat. Tyler the Creator and Bootsy Collins

THE WORLD

XXI · V.I.P. = Very Important Planet · THE WORLD

I wrote this book during a challenging year in my life, filled with ups and downs. Its creation was a journey that had its share of obstacles. While I felt happiness and pride in its progress, there were moments when I struggled to concentrate, and other times when everything flowed effortlessly. I personally experienced the profound meaning behind each Major Arcanum, which ultimately led to the completion of this work. Now, knowing it is in your hands and helping you gain a greater understanding is truly meaningful to me. I proudly dedicate the final Arcanum to this book, for it marks the end of the Tarot Wheel's cycle—the continuous journey that takes us from the Magician all the way round the World, the twenty-first Arcanum, and back round again and again—constantly evolving and advancing with every cycle. A bit like the mythical Ouroboros, the snake that symbolizes eternity by biting its own tail.

You may be asking yourself, "What happened to the Fool then?" Fear not! The answer is just after this chapter!

Where do we find the World in everyday life?

The World card represents individuals who have extensive connections, including celebrities and influencers. It includes people who have gained public recognition and possess the ability to reach far and wide with their endeavors, embodying their fame through the successful achievement of their goals. Those who lead highly social lives, have reached significant milestones, and are already gearing up for the next chapter can be represented by the World card. In contrast, when the card appears in reverse, it is associated with those who are not inclined toward social media, individuals who prefer to stay out of the spotlight or pursue their own ventures within their own circles.

Level of intensity of the World

Well, what can I say? This card is the essence of victory, glory, and the official recognition of having accomplished something truly magnificent—all for the world to see! And even when we take into account its potential drawbacks, there's really no need to worry excessively. It's actually quite manageable! So, I would rate its level of difficulty as a mere 2 out of 10.

The pros of the World

Finally, the long-awaited success of our journey is here! With the Judgment Arcanum, we gather the courage to step out and proudly proclaim our abilities. And with the World card, our choice to emerge from the shadows is not only rewarded but celebrated openly. This is where the official recognition comes into play, not only within our close-knit circle of people like family, friends, or partners but also from distant places as well. With this card, we should embrace limitless exploration and fame, without confining ourselves to any boundaries, be it geographical or otherwise. We have proven what we are capable of and are finally showcasing it.

I consider this a "bridge card" as it signifies a transition from reaching our goals to embarking on new beginnings. Think of the path that brought us here: starting with the spark of potential represented by the Magician, nurturing our ideas with the Empress, going through a period of growth and reflection with the Hanged Man, and now witnessing the completion of a significant cycle with the World—which marks the start and the end of a cycle—just like in life, completion is not the end but rather a new beginning. Hence, taking us back to the Magician, and so on. So, let's revel in our achievements, but also prepare for what lies ahead. With the World card, it's natural to become more vocal about our success, becoming our own advocates, connecting with others, and making ourselves known to as many people as possible. Embrace this victorious moment, enjoy the recognition you deserve, and get ready for the exciting new journey that awaits. Let's consider social media, for instance. The World card perfectly captures the essence of an influencer's work, allowing them to create a community of followers from all over, expanding their reach far beyond their place of origin. In terms of relationships, it resembles well-known couples who serve as role models for friends and family, enjoying a fulfilling and stable bond. For those who are single, the advice is to embrace new connections, perhaps through introductions from acquaintances, increasing the chances of meeting someone special. If Ms. Betty asks about work, emphasize the importance of building valuable connections for personal growth and job opportunities. The current team dynamics are harmonious, and it may even be a suitable time to consider a salary increase. Ask her if she feels fulfilled and what steps she can take to truly take flight and achieve her goals. What small actions can she take to make a significant impact?

The cons of the World

I find this card to be a bit of a "smooth operator" in a way: ultimately, in order to achieve certain milestones, we also need to know how to market ourselves and share a bit about who we are and what we do, just like the Magician (as I mentioned, there's a connection between these two cards!). However, when this card appears in reverse, we struggle to understand why pleasing others or sharing personal details should help us reach our goals. We either refuse to do it or face difficulties in opening up to the outside world. This card isn't particularly challenging (quite the opposite, actually!), so if you come across it in a reading, there's no need to worry too much about trying to change someone's approach. While it may cause them to miss out on opportunities, it doesn't seem ideal to force them into a pretense or modify their way of expression just to please others and put themselves in socially vulnerable positions without fully grasping the purpose behind it. It's not the same as the drawbacks of the High Priestess or the Hermit; rather, it signifies a milder form of withdrawal stemming from a lack of interest in engaging with others and building a network that supports our personal, professional, or social goals. This type of withdrawal ultimately hinders us from leveraging our connections to our advantage and may lead us to judge those who do. Do you know that feeling when you believe someone got a job through recommendation? Perhaps you could have been in their place, and it doesn't mean you lacked the skills for it! The right connections and abilities can definitely help in life, but it's a concept that feels distant from your way of thinking, especially with the reversed World card. In relationships, it brings to mind those individuals who have those cringe-worthy "couple profiles" on social media. We're talking about highly exclusive relationships or people who, once they get into a relationship or get married, tend to forget or neglect their friendships and turn their partnership into an impenetrable fortress. Single? It doesn't seem like the right time to open yourself up to new connections, even if your friends insist on introducing you to everyone in their phonebook, including distant cousins. When it comes to work, we struggle to build alliances, generally avoiding unnecessary conversations with colleagues. We arrive, do our tasks, and head back home without any particular ambitions or sparks of imagination. However, be cautious, because having the reversed World card or an unfavorable position isn't always entirely negative. Maybe it's time to shift our perspective and look at things from another point of view. The demands of social interactions can be draining, and we may not always have the resilience to navigate the chaos. Stepping back from worldly concerns could be the key to understanding if we're relying too much on past accomplishments and seeking external approval for our sense of fulfillment.

The World's advice

"Hey, Bae, want a table at the Ritz? Or an invite to Paris Hilton's party? All you need to do is ask! Being totally in the loop I can get privileged access to a seat at the table super-fast!"

A PLAYLIST FOR THE WORLD
We Are the Champions—Queen
The Final Countdown—Europe
Celebrate—Kool & the Gang
Good as Hell—Lizzo
Born to Run—Bruce Springsteen

SONGS FROM ITALY
Nessun Dorma—Giacomo Puccini

THE FOOL

0 · I'm cringe, but I'm free · THE FOOL

This is the chapter where I finally explain why it took me so long to tell you about the Fool, the zeroth Arcanum. But really, what was the rush? The fact that it comes at the end actually helps drive home the point that, just like its role as an outsider, the Fool doesn't play by the rules. Up until now, we've been following a set path, a journey that we discovered is cyclical and repeats itself from the Magician to the World. But here we stand face to face with an element that can pop up at any given moment, perhaps the true star of the Tarot's Wheel. Picture the rest of the Arcana as a kind of "Snakes and Ladders" game, and the Fool is the game piece! It's often misunderstood as having a negative connotation, but that's far from the truth. The Fool's lack of judgment, their readiness to follow any calling without any concern for personal gain, makes them almost divine. They are unburdened by ties, corruption, or compromises, and they welcome all ideas with open arms. If you think about it, the court jester (who can be associated with this Arcanum) was the only person close to royalty who could speak their mind freely, while laughing and jesting. This freedom translates into an unfiltered truth. And that's our Fool in a nutshell: genuine, childlike, innocent in their blissful ignorance of the compromises of life, randomly dressed, sometimes cringe-worthy (which can be embarrassing to those witnessing their carefree antics), but ultimately free from rules and conventions.

Where do we find the Fool in everyday life?

Have you ever seen the movie *Yes Man* with Jim Carrey? It tells the story of an individual with a rather dull and sad life who, at a certain point, meets a spiritual guru who convinces him to say "yes" to everything that comes his way. From the moment he accepts, he becomes the perfect embodiment of the Fool: he opens himself to any possibility or event without a plan or logical scheme, embracing whatever comes without a specific purpose, but simply for the joy of experiencing it. This card represents anyone who lives day by day on the spur of the moment and who wants to try everything at least once in life. Those who follow only their instincts and never reason, who become street performers and roam from one place to another, and those who have professions that involve pushing the boundaries of possibility—because it takes a good dose of madness and utopia to make the seemingly impossible possible.

The exploration associated with psychedelic states is something undertaken by those who can be associated with this Arcanum—I like to think that Albert Hofmann, who discovered LSD, was a Fool of his time. People who can be defined as eternal Peter Pans, who don't want or don't know how to grow up, who are unable to build anything around themselves, are associated with the unfavorable aspect of this card.

> **Jollyblu**
> What's the difference between the Magician and the Fool? Aren't they both representing youth or first times?

> **SoloRedie**
> The answer I like to give to this question, which I am often asked, is the following: the Magician is the Fool with a purpose or a project. It doesn't squander its potential but invests energy to make it come to fruition.

Level of intensity of the Fool

If not managed properly, the Fool can be a card with overwhelming and destructive energy. It takes the right amount of madness to break free from the rules and obligations of society but be careful not to go too far! That's why I give it an intensity rating of 8 out of 10.

The pros of the Fool

Since this card is quite unique in itself, we can draw some small parallels with other Major Arcana cards. For instance, with the Judgment card it shares a similar concept of taking a leap, but here, we do it blindly, like a bungee jump, with no former experience or awareness, nor with any purpose or profound lesson taken from it. We dive into the unknown solely for the thrill of the experience. On the other hand, with the Magician it shares the ability to dare and believe in an ideal, but while the Magician represents a person with ambition and a clear plan, the audacity and idealism of the Fool are somewhat purposeless. This card teaches us to appreciate the little joys that come our way. It plays a pivotal role in shaking up the occasionally rigid order in which we sometimes confine our lives. It encourages us to let go of inhibitions, at least once in a while.

If Ms. Betty is hoping that her new relationship will blossom into something beautiful and long-lasting, with this card in the spread, it suggests that she should perhaps learn to appreciate and fully enjoy the present moments they share rather than projecting herself too much into the future. It brings to mind the image of summer romances that burn bright but are short-lived. Conversely, if this card emerges in response to a question about an existing relationship, the guidance is to embrace new experiences and explore new activities, infusing a lighthearted and youthful energy to break free from monotony. There could also be the possibility of exploring an open relationship, allowing for connections with others to be considered.

When it comes to our career life, we can find ourselves being steered toward a path where we don't know where it leads to, yet it holds the promise of positive outcomes for our future. It would be worthwhile to have a conversation with Ms. Betty, asking her if she has ever contemplated leaving her current job and going freelance, especially if she feels that the current work environment is too restrictive for her true nature. Perhaps she could pluck up the courage to veer away from her current trajectory and embrace something entirely different, yet potentially more fulfilling. The advice is to embrace unconventional proposals that may initially appear peculiar, as they have the potential to lead us on a remarkable journey of self-discovery.

This card rewards originality and authenticity; there's no need to observe what others are doing in order to succeed. Express your creativity and your true character, even if they go against the current trends. Be true to yourself!

The cons of the Fool

The drawbacks of this Arcanum can manifest in two distinct ways, and they may even intertwine depending on the individual's level of self-awareness. On one hand, there is the fear of building illusions by following our instincts and true identity. It leads to living with unnecessary restraints, afraid to open up to new experiences and the unexpected. The person drawing this card tends to be quite rigid and leads an ordinary life because they fear embracing that spark of madness urging them to let go. They constantly feel the need to be in control of their direction and fail to see the value in trying something just for the sake of exploration. On the other hand, we may encounter individuals who are completely out of control. They go to extreme lengths to escape boredom and monotony, often failing to build a stable life because they constantly run away from responsibility as soon as they feel confined. There is a lack of self-awareness and a continuous desire to push past their limits, purely for the thrill of it. Interestingly, these two cases can be interconnected, as individuals of the first type may have had reckless experiences in the past or engaged with people who were like that. Having evolved beyond that lifestyle, they now perceive any impulsive decision or hint of freedom as a threat to their sense of stability.

This card carries the risk of impulsively rushing into actions without giving oneself the necessary time to reflect. It either stems from an underlying anxiety of having to have complete control over everything or an intense desire to engage in any activity whatsoever, just to avoid having nothing to do. Furthermore, it highlights an excess of idealism that clashes with the harsh realities of life.

This brings to mind the story of Christopher McCandless, who relinquished all his possessions in pursuit of a simple and authentic life in the untamed wilderness of Alaska, only to meet a tragic end due to a lack of proper planning and organization. His story is told in the movie *Into the Wild*, which I recommend.

But let's return to the Fool: when it comes to love and relationships, he's quite a disaster. His complete inability to commit leads him to approach everything as a constant cycle of "hit and run," distancing himself further and further from building something solid. In the workplace, he struggles to grasp the concept of subordination, making careers in highly structured environments or those requiring uniforms less suited for him. Since material possessions hold no interest for the Fool, it's important to be cautious about working without receiving fair compensation and to avoid indulging in extravagant expenses. Consider uninstalling apps like Amazon, Etsy, and any other shopping platforms on your phone—it's not the time to have loose spending habits.

This card urges us to constantly seek mental escape from reality. When faced with tests or interviews, we easily get distracted by the smallest things and begin to venture off on a tangent, leaving our conversation partner frustrated. We become the very cause of our own suffering. So, what advice or reflections does this unfavorable Arcanum offer? It is important to explore this with Ms. Betty and determine which of the two scenarios mentioned earlier resonates with her the most. What is her relationship with improvisation, and why does she find it so challenging to let go? What is the advantage of living on castles in the air without ever actually building something stable? Why is personal growth such a daunting task? Even Wonderland had its downsides, and constantly seeking relief in far-flung paradises, real or imagined, is not the optimal solution for a more fulfilling reality.

The Fool's advice

"Leaping from one idea to another without any logic? I'm all for it! Feeling youthful at 70? Count me in! Dyeing my hair a vibrant fluorescent pink outside of carnival season? Absolutely! Come along with me, and you won't experience a single dull moment."

A PLAYLIST FOR THE FOOL
Society—Eddie Vedder
It Takes a Fool to Remain Sane—The Ark
Freedom—George Michael
I Started a Joke—Bee Gees

SONGS FROM ITALY
Lo Voglio Fare—M¥SS KETA
Ballo, Ballo—Raffaella Carrà

If the Major Arcana cards were Tinder Dates

We have come to the finish line of our exploration of the Major Arcana. We have found out that they embody the complexities of human nature, as well as a variety of occupations. They embody the flaws and strengths inside of each of us, and their archetypal interpretations are part of our collective subconscious. In the current age, where we spend a substantial amount of time on social media and modern dating apps are a fundamental element of how we create connections and relationships, I have been thinking about how the Major Arcana would fit in this environment and which positive and negative patterns of behavior they would showcase in everyday life if they were to interact with one another and form relationships with each other.

The end result is truly surreal—you'll find yourself, your exes, casual flings that were over in a flash, those you have ghosted, and those that drove you crazy. Put together, it's the cards of the Major Arcana as Tinder dates.

THE MAGICIAN: They're hyperactive, flirting with anything that moves, constantly glued to their phone, and familiar with every social media platform known to mankind. They'll promise you the moon and the stars, but then conveniently blame a misunderstanding and vanish from your life like a puff of smoke.

THE HIGH PRIESTESS: They always know what you're about to say before you even open your mouth. They despise sunbathing and insist on buying a gazebo to go to the beach. They constantly want you to spend time with their cats and refuse to leave the house unless they have done at least two hours of yoga and meditation. They'll leave you because they prefer to be alone.

THE EMPRESS: As soon as you meet, they start calling you "sweetie" and "baby-kins" in public. They ask you to unfollow all your exes and insist on creating a couple's profile on Facebook. They only send heart-eyed emojis on WhatsApp because it's the only way they know how to communicate. Their house is Instagram-worthy, and their favorite phrase is "Cover up, you'll catch a cold."

THE EMPEROR: They have a TikTok profile where they show themselves working out to forget their ex. They have a tribal tattoo on their bicep. They claim to be self-made, having thrown themselves among the wolves and emerged as the alpha. They will refer to you as "their latest conquest," and they certainly make a good impression when you introduce them to your friends because they are very attractive.

THE HIEROPHANT: They want to introduce you to their family on the second date, they wear a purity ring, and they can't wait to see you in their mother's wedding dress. On the first date, they take you on a tour of their favorite churches or to a nice Sunday lunch with all their friends, most of whom are cousins. A bit old-fashioned, but definitely a catch. Solid, I would say.

THE LOVERS: They have four ongoing relationships and have no intention of ending any of them. When it comes to choosing where to meet, they always leave the decision up to you. Make sure you have the evening free because if you go out for dinner, it will take them eight hours to decide between the appetizer and the main course.

THE CHARIOT: You won't find them where you last left them; you'll probably meet up between a safari in Namibia and an adventure trip to Iceland. Their most frequently used hashtag? Naturally, #wanderlust. When people ask them what they do for a living, they describe themselves as a digital nomad, even though they haven't quite figured out what that really means.

STRENGTH: They have a tattoo that says "Power Is Nothing Without Control," they're into bodybuilding, and insist on carrying the new furniture upstairs without using the elevator. They're a natural motivator, and after a month of dating, you'll find yourself enrolled in three different gyms where they have a premium membership. At their place, all the fabrics have a safari print.

THE HERMIT: You'll only see them far in the distance if you shine a torchlight on them; if you want to spend time with them, you'll have to follow them on their endless mountain treks. Slow as molasses, every time you need to do something practical, they spend hours thinking about how to do it right. They'll show up to the date dressed as Gandalf the Grey and only talk about Tolkien's books and how they've improved their existence.

THE WHEEL OF FORTUNE: They are the most unpredictable individual you could think of; you never know if they'll call you back, so be prepared for a roller coaster ride. They can be the most fun person you've ever met, but also the most pessimistic, depending on how they wake up. They dream of taking you to Las Vegas to gamble at the casinos and then marry you (and run away with the winnings).

JUSTICE: Regardless of the topic, they always want to be right and are ready to pull out the criminal code to back up their claims. They never shy away from telling you the truth, even if it's something you don't want to hear, and they know exactly how to hit your sore spots. They're court TV show enthusiasts, never missing an episode, and they'll give you a hard time if you board the bus without a ticket.

THE HANGED MAN: They're experts in ghosting and they love anything that involves ropes. You'll have to accompany them to Shibari classes on weekends and let yourself be tied and suspended as their practice dummy. They spend money like water as they hold the world record for how fast they can spend their paycheck the moment it hits their account.

DEATH: On your first date, they start sharing all their traumas with you. They only go out at night to dance to dark wave music, and their hair is a different color every day. Their favorite show is *Extreme Makeover*, and if they get angry, you'll be the receiver of the silent treatment like you've never known it before.

TEMPERANCE: A connoisseur of natural water brands with a past as a bartender, they only take you to trendy venues where dinner is enjoyed in silence. They speak at an almost imperceptible volume, and their favorite phrase is "Yes, but calm down," which only manages to make you even more annoyed. They take two hours to get ready, yet still show up looking plain and simple.

THE DEVIL: As soon as you start dating, they want to get everyone you know into bed with them—your mother, your father, and even your extended family, including the ones by marriage. They're obsessed with online trading and try to get you to invest in cryptocurrencies. Whatever they earn, they spend it on impulsive shopping. They take you to BDSM parties, where you unexpectedly discover that you enjoy yourself.

THE TOWER: You step into their place and find out they're a hardcore hoarder: no tidying up, just piles of stuff ready to topple with the slightest breeze, and they proudly call it their "creative chaos." They always hit you up at the eleventh hour and get all worked up if you don't tag along on their wild (mis)adventures. When it comes to "Jenga" or "Shanghai," they beat you at it badly.

THE STAR: Their favorite date? Going to the garden center every Sunday to buy yet another plant they'll love more than you. You can't tell if they're crazy or just pretending, but they bid farewell by shouting "Stellar kisses!" And if you're not into *au naturel*, no beach adventures for you two.

THE MOON: A typical "mama bear"—the placenta jewelry crafting type. They know everything about you. How? Well, it's simple: they spy on you while you sleep, read your messages while you're in the shower, and dig into every little detail of your life, even those secret childhood diaries (with your mother's cooperation, no less). And when they uncover something, they'll tell you they had a dream about you cheating on them, just to get you to spill the beans.

THE SUN: Always high-spirited, perhaps a bit too much. They went to beach parties with their entourage of inseparable friends, and you'll find yourself constantly in their presence even during intimate moments. They exclusively wear the Desigual brand and their favorite colors are yellow and orange. They suggest a trip together, but you soon discover it'll be a hitchhiking adventure.

JUDGMENT: They scrutinize you from head to toe every time you meet, silently passing judgment. In their car, only loud music blares, with their favorite track being "Mr. Saxobeat." The excessively dramatic sound of their alarm clock is the trumpet blast from Beethoven's Fifth Symphony.

THE WORLD: They always know everything about everyone, they're the king/queen of gossip. They studied public relations and work as an event organizer. When you go out together, they spend 90 percent of the time talking to anyone but you, and then they send you a WhatsApp message to make up for it.

THE FOOL: On your birthday, they give you a bungee jumping experience as a gift, but only because they actually want to do it themselves. The day after you've been intimate, they have already forgotten about you.

Spreads and Methods of Tarot reading

At this point, you already know how to navigate through the meanings of different Major Arcana cards and feel the desire to try your hand at Tarot reading, especially to understand how to lay out the cards, how relevant their positions are, how to determine the appropriate number of cards to use, and so on. Are you curious to learn all of this? This is the right chapter! But first, I quickly want to address a question I received on Instagram, as the answer might also be helpful to you.

Confused99
When I lay out the cards, how do I figure out who's doing what? Like, when there are two people involved in a situation, how do I know which one is taking which action? It's all so confusing, and I'm worried that I won't be able to find the right answer!

SoloRedie
Alright, let's not panic, one question at a time. First of all, assign roles to each card you draw. If you have two people involved, it's quite simple: the first card can represent person 1, and the second card can represent person 2. If there are multiple people involved, read the cards for each individual and discover the influence that each of them can have on the same situation.

Let's start with the basics: A spread is the layout or pattern in which we arrange the Tarot cards when we need to read them. It helps us give a chronological order to the cards, make sense of what we see, and establish a thread that leads us from the beginning of the situation to its conclusion. For a Tarot reading, you can use a well-known spread or create one on the spot, depending on the querent's question.

First of all, before we start reading the cards, let's determine how many cards we need. Perhaps two is a bit too few, as you risk falling in the trap of making associations. You know, those pairings you find in books that tell you the Empress is always a woman, and the Hermit is an elderly person. Let's be honest, Bae, we've looked them up at one point, maybe on the internet. So, let's avoid spreads with only two cards because they also provide little depth and dimension to your reading.

Shall we start with three cards? That seems like a good number. We can use the storytelling technique to read our spread, which means we can create a smooth and continuous sequence using the images, as if we were starting a story. But if you find it too challenging at first, you can assign roles to each card. Let me give you a few examples:

1: Past / 2: Present / 3: Future

1: Person 1 / 2: Person 2 / 3: Ongoing Situation

1: Ongoing Situation / 2: Advised Action / 3: Solution

1: Action / 2: Pros / 3: Cons

This role-playing tactic is not exclusive to the three-card spread; you can use it regardless of the number of Tarot cards you decide to draw. And just like in theater, you need to assign roles to each position before laying out the cards. Once you have listened to the question, clearly explain to Ms. Betty what the cards you position on the table indicate to give her the answer to her question.

When you become more proficient with three cards, you can move on to four. You can lay them horizontally if the question relates to a sequence of action, for instance, if it represents steps to be taken or an action that unfolds over time. You can place them in a cross shape, from bottom to top, if they represent a situation involving a second person and we want to see the dynamics between them. And you can lay them vertically if, for example, we are talking about an improvement or a gesture that starts from a spontaneous inclination and then becomes a more rational action, and so on and so forth.

THE CROSS SPREAD—a method that holds a special place in my heart as it was taught to me by Stella Noctis, my cherished mentor—is remarkably adaptable and lends itself well to different situations. It also offers an opportunity for storytelling, as you can opt to read the cards in a way that follows their natural flow, intertwining their meanings and creating a captivating narrative. Below, you'll find the diagram depicting the proper order of the cards, accompanied by the respective roles that can be assigned to each. It's important to note that each role represents an alternative, and not all meanings are simultaneously attributed to every individual card.

1: Person 1 / 2: Person 2 / 3: Situation / 4: Resolution

1: Past / 2: Present / 3: Resolution at 2-3 months / 4: Resolution at 5-6 months

1: Impulsive Action / 2: Block / 3: Opportunity / 4: Rational Thought

Tip: Once you've interpreted a spread, don't just stop at what you initially see, but revisit each card to grasp the meanings that come to you gradually. Observe how the Arcana interact with each other and consider the numerology aspect of each card as well.

Let me explain: If the number of cards that come up is increasing, it means that in this situation, there is an evolution moving forward, a growth taking place. If a reading consists only of Major Arcana cards up to number XI, the energy at play is young and in need of development. Conversely, if we have Arcana cards from XII to XXI, it represents a more mature energy. If there is a mix of these numbers, there is likely greater awareness of certain aspects, but work still needs to be done on others.

When it comes to the position of the cards, if you're using the storytelling technique, the card at the bottom can represent something that tends to be done impulsively because it symbolizes the foundation, the core. On the other hand, the card at the top can represent something approached rationally because it represents the mind. It's necessary to try different combinations to challenge ourselves and gain our own experience. Anyone can perform a reading by memorizing the keywords associated with each card. The trick to becoming an excellent card reader is to use the cards to create a narrative that speaks to the story of the person seeking guidance in a complete and personal manner, connecting all the pieces, and explaining them in a way that truly resonates with the querent, creating a unique and meaningful experience! We must practice flexibility to avoid finding ourselves in complex situations that we don't know how to handle. Feeling comfortable during a reading is fundamental, and we will delve deeper into this concept when we discuss the ethics of card reading.

HOW TO MAKE YOUR OWN SPREADS

Let's move on to the practical part. We won't need any white glue or rounded-tip scissors, but we will require a sufficient amount of rationality, intuition, and a willingness to offer solutions to Ms. Betty's problems.

As I mentioned earlier, the spreads you create can be especially useful for specific questions or moments in life, such as lunar phases, different strategies to achieve a goal, an opportunity to clarify something that causes confusion, and so on.

The first element to consider is how to answer these fundamental questions: What is my spread about? What can it be used for? What type of questions can it answer?

· What are we talking about? Work, feelings, relationships, or personal aspects?

· How many people are involved?

· Is the spread general or regarding a specific topic?

· Are there any options or steps to be taken in this particular situation?

The second important element is the shape you will give your spread.

· *V shape/horseshoe shape:* Useful for questions that involve doubt, a crossroads, or two paths to choose from.

· *Step/sequence shape:* Serves to outline the necessary steps toward a goal. You can add additional cards outside the layout to represent potential obstacles to watch out for, antagonists (people or situations), untapped potential that you may not have considered, and so on.

· *Circular/round shape:* Suitable for general spreads when faced with the classic situation where someone says, "I don't know what to ask, you decide" (the worst thing to say to a card reader!).

· *Square shape:* Used when you want to observe how two situations reflect or mirror each other.

It goes without saying that if you wish to create spreads in the shape of a sun, heart, or tree, feel free to unleash your imagination as long as the shape serves the interpretation. You can also take a look at the spreads found in this book to understand their dynamics and find inspiration.

Establishing the direction and, above all, the starting point is essential. If you create your own spreads, you can indicate the role of each card and the reading order with a number that determines which Arcanum to start with and which one to end with.

Pignol_u
Hi Redie, is it okay to draw an extra card for advice? In this case, when I lay out the cards, where should I place it?

SoloRedie
Absolutely okay! The advice card can be the summary of the entire situation you are analyzing, an additional detail that further helps clarify ideas and try to recommend the best course of action to solve Ms. Betty's dilemma. As it is an extra card, I suggest placing it outside your layout or as the last card.

Read your own cards, Bae!

At the beginning of a Tarot study journey, self-reading can be a good way to practice and see how the cards respond. However, it's common (and perfectly normal) to experience moments where, especially in the beginning, when we turn the cards, all that comes to mind is a resounding "What is this?!" We may feel disoriented by readings that we perceive as either overly positive or overly negative. But what if the results were actually accurate, and it was indeed we who were seeing everything as excessively positive or excessively negative?

Self-conditioning often becomes the most misleading factor, as one of the most challenging aspects of a reading is to be objective, transcending our own self and self-awareness, and observing ourselves from an outside perspective as a complete stranger.

When we engage in self-analysis and expose ourselves to self-reflection, various elements come into play, such as expectations, excessive or complete lack of self-criticism, and the inability to envision ourselves in any role other than our own. These are all complex situations to unravel, so don't worry if you can't do it right away! Learning to see ourselves from the outside-in is not an easy skill to master. For those who are used to practicing it, starting with a short meditation can be helpful.

Now I'll reveal my secrets for a top-notch self-reading. They're not foolproof, but so far, they have yielded the desired results, both for myself and my students, as well as for all the people I've given these tips to. You find them here, at the end of the journey through the Major Arcana for two reasons: the first is related to knowledge of the cards and having become familiar with their meanings, and the second is because, with the Judgment card, we've learned to overcome the "impostor syndrome" and gained more confidence in ourselves. Consequently, reading the cards on our own is also a way to take the plunge and be certain that we have enough experience to do so. There are six steps, all useful, but Bae, the sixth one is truly essential!

Here goes!

ADVICE #1 · **Be impartial.** This means refraining from favoring either yourself or the opposing party, even if the latter seems less likely. While it's natural to desire a favorable outcome in a given situation, it's important to resist the urge to root for someone else, if that's the case! How can you achieve this? One approach is to write down the situation or question on a sheet of paper and read it as if it were an extract of a book or a math problem. Your task is to find a solution to that problem, rather than getting caught up in it as if you were watching a soap opera. Remember, don't take sides! Stay unbiased.

ADVICE #2 · **Trust your intuition.** Yes, I know you may have come across this advice in other books or on the internet, but let me assure you, it's wisdom worth heeding because it holds true. Call it intuition, call it a sixth sense, use whichever term resonates with you. That inner voice is eagerly waiting to emerge. Place your trust in what you sense and observe laid out on the table before you. Often, the belief that we cannot read Tarot cards is simply an illusion. Pay close attention to the cards, study the imagery, seek to understand the messages they convey, and take it one Arcanum at a time. Then, carefully analyze the overall situation, observing how the cards interact and influence one another, and truly grasp how they connect with you. Delve deep into the essence of each meaning and analyze how it echoes within the situation you have posed as a question. One method to hone your intuition can be reading without a specific question in mind: shuffle the cards and draw one. Allow your subconscious to connect with that Arcanum freely and effortlessly. Grasp what resonates with you and let go of the rest. Embrace the guidance that card has to offer you without questioning why that particular one emerged instead of another. Strive to practice as often as possible and work on accepting what the deck presents to you, without objecting or thinking that you drew the wrong card.

ADVICE #3 · **Don't complicate life for yourself,** as it's already complex enough on its own. Avoid creating overly intricate patterns, especially if you're just starting out (we've already discussed this in the chapter dedicated to spreads). As you gain more confidence in self-reading, you can begin to practice with spreads you create for others. But until then, maintain a low profile and strive to simplify your existence. We seek solutions to our problems, not additional complications!

ADVICE #4 · **Repeat the question.** Using the question as if it were a mantra will help you focus on it and not on the expectations surrounding the answer. Personally, shifting the attention away from the situation itself and onto the preparation of the reading helps me a lot because I imagine the protagonist of that dynamic, and the dynamic itself, as if they belong to a book rather than something affecting me personally. Pretend to be unfamiliar with yourself and don't take for granted that you know everything. You have a lot to learn about something you think you already know. "I know that I know nothing," the maxim attributed to Socrates, can accompany you on this endeavor.

ADVICE #5 · **Stick to the topic.** Remember those times in class when you were writing essays, and the teacher would tell you that you had lost your train of thought? It would leave you feeling disheartened because you thought that including all that content would guarantee you a good grade. Well, that's precisely what I'm talking about. Some situations call for more words, while others require fewer. Try to recognize when you're going off on a tangent, taking the reading in directions unrelated to the initial topic. In a nutshell, don't overcomplicate things; stick to the main idea.

ADVICE #6 · **Accept what you see.** Under no circumstances whatsoever should you repeat a reading on the same question just because you're not pleased with what came up or because the answer doesn't align with your expectations. It's a lack of respect toward yourself, Tarot, and your intuition. It's simply not the way to go! Instead, work with what has surfaced, whether it's positive or not. And let me tell you, if you decide to go off on your own and try to test the cards anyway, or if you come across a stubborn Ms. Betty who insists on asking you the same question in different forms, you'll soon realize that the deck won't take responsibility for its actions. It will play games with you, showing the same cards over and over again or presenting increasingly confusing and contradictory cards. So stick to the first reading. That's the way to go!

So, let's repeat together: be impartial, trust your intuition, don't complicate life, repeat the question, stick to the topic, and accept what you see. Great! Now that you know my secrets, you're good to go and self-analyze thoroughly like they do with urine samples in a lab (forgive the analogy—it's the first one that came to mind, sorry).

Emp-Ress

Hello, Redie! There's something I've been wanting to ask you for a while, but I haven't had the courage. When I told a friend that I read Tarot cards for myself, she told me to stop because it brings bad luck. She shared a story about someone who read their own cards and never found a boyfriend, and now I'm afraid the same thing might happen to me. Should I take her advice?

SoloRedie

Your friend has cooked up a mixture of urban legends, superstitions, and a touch of relationship anxiety. When it comes to matters of the heart, I don't believe that Tarot cards have any influence on someone's single status, unless that person was chasing potential partners away by constantly threatening them with readings. Perhaps she simply isn't interested in having a boyfriend at all. Let's consider that case closed. As for bad luck, I won't even entertain the idea. Supporting this theory with concrete evidence would be challenging, and I don't think our misfortunes can be attributed to the times we've picked up our decks for a good, well-deserved reading. Tarot cards are an incredible tool for self-analysis. They allow us to better understand ourselves and decipher potential developments in a situation, taking into consideration who we are and how we tend to act. Keep doing your self-readings, continue exploring your inner self, and tell your friend that maybe she needs to give Tarot cards a try as well. Seeing is believing!

One last piece of advice: try keeping a sort of "logbook" or journal. At the beginning of each day, draw a card, observe it, try to understand what it may be telling you, and write down some keywords in your journal. In the evening, review what you have written and compare it to what happened during the day. See if there is any correlation between the events and the drawn Arcanum and evaluate whether the advice it provided was helpful. By doing this, you'll have a continuous feedback loop on the accuracy and practicality of the cards you draw along your journey. Additionally, your ability to listen and gather the advice from the cards will improve over time.

The art of Storytelling

One of the things that people most often recognize in me is the ability to tell readings as if I've known their stories forever, for the wealth of details I can provide them with and for the vividness of the images I'm able to evoke. Presented this way, this chapter may seem self-celebratory, and while on one hand I always strive to remain modest, on the other hand, I'm simply stating an objective truth (also because I'm the first to constantly seek feedback from those who get their cards read, precisely because I don't imagine anything, I stick to what they tell me, and I simply seek confirmation from the person involved). So, what's my secret then? Lots of practice. I channel my intuition and master the art of storytelling, which is the ability to construct a narrative starting with the images.

But what exactly is storytelling? This term has gained significant popularity in recent years, particularly in the world of digital communication. It is a renowned technique that effectively captures the attention and interest of potential consumers by narrating a compelling story around a product or service.

But how can we apply this approach to explaining the meanings of the Arcana that emerge in a reading? As always, Bae, I'll try to give you some advice, but feel free to experiment with steps that perhaps I haven't mentioned but that you deem functional for this purpose. The more strategies you develop and test, the greater the likelihood of delivering an outstanding reading that resonates as much as possible with Ms. Betty's situation.

ADVICE #1 · Create a sense of depth. Imagine that a reading is like a painting or a sculpture. Just as with any artwork, it all starts with an idea, a concept, a rough sketch that serves as the foundation for the final masterpiece. Now, let's apply this to our reading. Take a close look at the cards that have appeared and extract the keywords they convey through their vivid imagery, the initial thoughts, and symbols they evoke. Communicate them out aloud, let them come to life. Then dive deeper into each Arcanum, exploring their intricate details. For example, in the deck you're using, does the Hermit hold a lantern? Where is it pointing? What does it make you think of? And the Hanged Man, symbolizing a purposeful discomfort, but doesn't its posture also hint at a period of gestation? What does our dear Ms. Betty need to nurture and bring forth? Is it an idea? A project? Remember, connecting with the cards takes time, so take all the time you need. Lastly, incorporate your insights based on the feedback you've received during your meaningful exchange with the person in front of you.

ADVICE #2 · **The reading must be multidimensional.** Even though Tarot cards are laid out on a flat surface and sometimes even in a sequential order, they come to life in your hands (thanks to your interpretation) and gain depth and complexity. This applies to revisiting the concepts you've already explained as well. Even if your cards represent the past, present, and immediate future, I suggest going back to the earlier cards to see if there's anything else to add. The cards influence one another: what happened in the past shapes our actions in the present, and how the present unfolds provides insights for shaping our future. So, there's no strict, one-way timeline. Taking a step back allows you to examine triggering factors, the context in which the person seeking the reading is moving, and the resources available to them. These are crucial details that can truly make a difference. Just as you allow your interpretation to come alive in three dimensions, don't underestimate this advice—it might reveal things you initially overlooked. Don't be in a hurry to wrap up a reading, because it takes time to avoid making assumptions about certain interpretations.

ADVICE #3 · **Pay attention to how the Arcana interact with each other.** Mastering the meanings of each individual card is crucial, but the real game-changer is observing the order in which the cards pop up. Are they in numerical order? If they are, it means this reading might be showing an evolution or progression of the situation. We're heading toward growth, even if some cards are playing it upside down, and the path ahead is brimming with hints for self-improvement. Now, if the numbers on the cards seem all over the place, pay attention to the ones with the lowest and highest numbers. Let me illustrate it for you: let's say we have the Two of Cups, King of Pentacles, Five of Pentacles, and Seven of Wands in a reading. The cards with the lowest numbers highlight aspects that need our focus and room for improvement, while the ones with the highest numbers represent already established aspects that we must value and use to our advantage. The same applies, of course, to the Major Arcana. Another way to observe their interaction is through the interplay of masculine and feminine energies: Do we have more cards from one gender or another? Is there a balance or a clear contrast? In the cards depicting anthropomorphic figures, even their gazes can hold significance: Are they facing each other or turning their backs? Are we moving toward that energy or leaving it behind? Each card has an individual meaning, but when considered within the context it emerged, it can provide us with a wealth of additional information!

ADVICE #4 · **Pay attention to common characteristics.** As you have seen in the profiles dedicated to the Major Arcana (and as you will also see in the Minor Arcana), there are cards that share similar characteristics. At first glance, they may appear similar, but when you look closer, you can see the differences. It's like when you enthusiastically wave at someone in the distance you think you know but as they approach, you realize they're not the person you thought (so you end up waving to a mysterious person behind them to cover up the gaffe).

For instance, both the Magician and the World card speak of communication, so they share this aspect in common. The King of Wands may vaguely resemble the Emperor. The High Priestess and the Moon work with intuitive energies, while Death and the Wheel bring about changes. Take a look at your reading and try to grasp if there's a common thread among the cards, to get a sense if there's a shared theme or something that easily catches your eye, giving you a broad understanding of which needs emerge more prominently. If you're using the Minor Arcana, you can take a look at the suits: is one suit more dominant than the others? Well, that points to a clear theme that needs addressing, and each individual card offers detailed insights into how to approach it and the specific subtopics it encompasses. Do you notice multiple "celestial bodies" in your reading, like the Sun and the Moon or the Moon and the Star? What does this emphasis bring to mind? Mastering the meanings of the Arcana and gaining experience through a wide range of readings will help you develop a memory of the various instances where common characteristics have provided specific interpretations for groups of cards that you can conveniently group together. A useful exercise could be to create a handbook where you can note keywords such as "change," "introspection," "assertion," and "socialization," and list the Major and Minor Arcana cards that can be associated with each of these themes. Besides aiding in memorization, these techniques provide immediate prompts to recognize the theme of a particular reading based on the number of cards with common concepts that emerge together.

ADVICE #5 · **Pay attention to the differences.** Now, this is a bit of the opposite of the previous advice because while I suggested looking for similarities earlier, I'm now asking you to look for differences. In a spread, which card is the "black sheep"? Which card stands out from the rest and what message does it convey? The difference might manifest as a reversed card amidst upright ones. Take a moment to understand why it's there and why it's not necessarily a bad thing. Maybe it's meant to bring Ms. Betty back down to earth or serve as a warning about the risks of taking certain favorable dynamics for granted. Those upright cards can make her feel invincible, but this different one adds a dose of caution. Differences can also arise in numbers. So, if all the cards in a spread are in ascending order, but the last one has a lower number, it signifies an aspect that could lead to regression or signals a revision of something we haven't fully considered. Here's an exercise for you: try doing quick spreads without a specific question, and keenly observe the odd one on the table. Analyze how it differs from the other cards, whether it plays the role of an antagonist or a warning, and brainstorm ways to reconcile it with the rest of the cards. Imagine advice and constructive interpretations tailored specifically to it.

ADVICE #6 · **Don't fantasize, aim for clarity.** Storytelling is a powerful tool that allows you to dive deep into the heart of the situation and deliver a reading that truly stands out. But be careful not to get carried away and embellish it too much, letting your imagination run wild. It's easy to get caught up in a specific situation and force meanings onto certain cards just because they remind us of something we've personally experienced or a reading similar to the one we're doing now. Stay grounded and focused on the present. This is how we could end up putting ourselves into what we see but in the wrong way. Always remember that when it comes to Tarot, your key role is like that of a simultaneous interpreter (I don't say this to diminish you, it's a very noble role!) and as such, your task is to let the cards speak their own truth, not based on your personal assumptions or inclinations. This is why in a reading, I prefer to say "based on what I see" or "based on the cards that have come up" rather than "in my opinion," precisely because the interpretation I provide is grounded in the drawn cards, not on my own assumption.

Another important aspect of storytelling is the clarity and ease with which we reach the heart of Ms. Betty.

We should use simple terms, short and impactful sentences, and practical examples that help her grasp the advice we want to convey in our reading. The more straightforward you are, the more direct the message becomes! Let's leave fancy words, lengthy sentences, and convoluted metaphors to egocentric and confusing Tarot readers. We're down-to-earth and pragmatic! We prefer readings that are crystal clear and conceptually accessible to a wide range of people.

Tarot and Ethics or "things we don't think about but should"

Reading Tarot cards is a fascinating, exploratory, introspective practice, but above all, remember that it should be healthy and enjoyable. For this reason, the recommendations I give you in this chapter may sound like a little parental advice (yes, you can say it: I sound a bit like the Hierophant), but they absolutely need to be kept in mind. In order to maintain the character qualities I listed above, the first piece of advice I feel compelled to give you is as follows: if you're not feeling well, if you feel tired, if the energy you get from the person in front of you is not positive, then **DO NOT READ THE CARDS**. Readings are an intimate exchange in which each person involved must feel comfortable. If you are not sufficiently clear-headed, you might find yourself struggling, or you may be in a situation of particular vulnerability due to your health or tiredness and feel drained of energy once the consultation is over. Instead, reschedule the appointment or politely decline the request that is being made of you.

When it comes to the Tarot, no one should ever feel obligated to do anything! The same goes for when we come across someone who has expressed skepticism about the divinatory practice but is being pressured by others to have their cards read. We're not circus performers, and we don't need to prove anything. Our purpose isn't to convince those who don't believe in this method. Besides, belief is subjective, and Tarot is not a religion.

Regarding compensation, it is only fair to ask for something in return. If you're just starting out and don't feel comfortable asking for monetary compensation, you can suggest exchanging your time for services, food/drinks, or whatever you prefer. For example, if you read for someone who studies palmistry or astrology, you can in turn ask for a consultation. As I mentioned earlier, readings are an exchange, so even though you may love reading Tarot cards, don't do it for nothing. You are offering your time, your efforts, your expertise, and your studies, and it's important to give value to all of that.

The cards aren't a magic fix for other people's problems and practicing with them isn't mandatory. That's why, during a reading, while you do have a responsibility to offer some guidance on how to harness the energies tied to the cards that come up, it cannot replace the need for proper therapy. So, I strongly advise that in cases of severe distress, you suggest seeking assistance from a professional—always in a discreet and respectful manner.

For the same reason, it's recommended not to repeat the consultation within a period of three months. This allows time for the situation to develop and for the client to take necessary actions to make changes. As I mentioned earlier, if someone becomes persistent and contacts you the following week to have their cards read again, it's best to politely decline. An important aspect to consider in this field is the issue of dependency on Tarot cards. The idea of being able to get a little glimpse into the actions related to a specific aspect of our life can be helpful if used in the right way. That means working on our weaknesses and striving to be the best version of ourselves in that situation. However, it can also be quite tempting if we tend to get too comfortable and not take action, hoping that things will just magically fall into place, or if we believe that our life solely depends on what others do (you'll notice this when Ms. Betty asks about an ex: "Will they come back to me?"). This can lead us to constantly wanting to predict other people's moves, or curiosity can drive us to keep looking at that same thing over and over again, without taking an active stance. If you feel that someone might develop such a dependency and is relying on the cards to solve things on their behalf, make sure to raise their awareness of this and take control of the situation as soon as possible. It's important to experiment, make mistakes, and learn to take action. The cards have their limitations if they are used as the absolute truth and sole perspective on our world rather than as a guidance tool.

Speaking of this, another fundamental aspect is to avoid asking the same question multiple times. This applies even to self-readings. Tarot knows when we're seeking different answers to the same question a thousand times, and, playfully, it will shuffle out random cards or consistently show the same Arcanum. Taking care of your deck also means respecting it, not subjecting it—and yourself—to this kind of stress. When we read the cards, we must try not to judge the person in front of us or the situation we are analyzing because the main focus is on the deck. We, as readers, are merely the conduit between the deck and Ms. Betty, a kind of translator between "Tarot language" and everyday language. It requires a great capacity for detachment, which is achieved by training ourselves to temporarily suppress our ego and what we think we know, especially if a particular issue reminds us of something we have personally experienced.

We shouldn't hastily jump to simplistic conclusions. It's important to keep in mind that each situation is unique, even if we find some points of connection with the person involved. This aspect becomes particularly significant when we read Tarot cards for a friend, someone we believe we know inside out. When they entrust us with their concerns, they're placing a small part of their life in our hands. Therefore, it's crucial to approach it with respect and avoid projecting our own thoughts or actions onto their situation. Stay focused on what the cards reveal instead.

Showing respect to the person in front of us also means seeking their feedback on what we are saying. Our responsibility is to speak the truth, but we should be mindful of how we communicate it. Words are important. In Italy, there was a well-known card reader named Nascia Prandi, who gained notoriety for her less-than-diplomatic approach. However, if we were to replicate her methods, we would bear the responsibility for the distress the person would carry with them after our reading. Furthermore, it's likely they wouldn't be pleased to see us again.

Don't expect praise in the feedback; we're not taking part in a competition where we have to guess what's going on in the mind of the person in front of us. Instead, we should focus on actively listening and understanding how we can use those elements to offer a precise and relevant interpretation to our interlocutor.

Keep in mind that the vulnerability tied to the trust the querent is placing in you is valuable and deserves respect. So, refrain from taking liberties that haven't been granted to you. Tarot readers act as advisors, but they should also exhibit impartiality. That's why it's crucial to communicate the truth with a gentle yet firm approach, without sugarcoating it, even if the situation revealed by the cards doesn't meet Ms. Betty's expectations.

As you continue to develop your practice, you'll discover the appropriate words and approach to convey the messages of the Arcana. Strive to use simple and understandable language, avoiding lengthy detours into philosophical metaphors or intricate details. Keep your communication clear and relatable, steering clear of profanity (though I must admit, I occasionally slip up—my apologies). If such a slip happens, I always ask the person in front of me to "excuse my French." Lastly, maintain a comforting tone of voice that instills reassurance rather than foreboding any unnecessary drama.

Tired99

Hey Ali, I wanted to chat with you about something. So, I did this Tarot card reading at an event, but let me tell you, afterwards my head was pounding, and I was in such a foul mood. I did readings for like five hours straight and completely lost track of time! Any advice you can give me for next time? Thanks a bunch!

SoloRedie

I'm sorry to hear that your last experience didn't turn out well! Reading Tarot cards at events should be a fun and enlightening time for you. It's a chance to challenge yourself with different questions and make a name for yourself, and you should be taking away fond memories, not a pounding headache! Look, next time make sure you arrive well-rested. And if that's not possible, make a prior arrangement with the organizers for a shorter time slot; personally, I try not to go beyond three hours per session. Take short breaks of around ten minutes after serving a certain number of people. Use that time to hydrate, take a breather, and recharge your batteries a bit. I know it can be tough to take breaks when you're caught up in the event's intensity, the concentration, and the adrenaline rush, but remember, your well-being comes first. Plus, taking occasional breaks ensures you maintain the quality of your readings! Avoid alcohol, as you'll need to be as sharp and focused as possible. Since you're at an event, it's best to steer clear of touchy or personal topics that could affect your own emotions. Remember, reading the cards is all about energy exchange and requires your constant attention. If you're low on energy or feel drained, you'll end up feeling depleted once the experience is over. As you attend more events, you'll find that things will get better. Good luck out there.

The 56 cards of the (far from minor) Minor Arcana

It was so much fun coming up with alternative names for the Major Arcana. Since they represent archetypes with broad meanings, I associated them with song lyrics, idioms, popular images from movies, and memorable quotes. On the other hand, the Minor Arcana don't have symbolic names, but they are named based on the combination of the number and corresponding suit.

The Minor Arcana is divided into four suits: Wands, Cups, Swords, and Pentacles (sometimes called Coins). If these concepts sound familiar to you, it's probably because you've played *Briscola* or *Scopa* at least once in your life. You can find them in Napoletane and Piacentine decks.

Each suit consists of cards numbered from one to ten, totaling 40 numeral cards. Some decks depict them similar to regular playing cards, with the suit symbol multiplied by the number (these are called pips). Others, like the Rider-Waite-Smith deck and its variations, feature allegorical illustrations that capture their essence. The interpretation of these 40 cards is influenced by the symbolic value of their corresponding numbers and the subtle nuances of the element associated with each suit—so they can also be seen as Fire, Water, Air, or Earth. The remaining 16 cards, known as the Court cards, consist of the Page (sometimes called the Knave), Knight, Queen, and King.

The Minor Arcana typically depict down-to-earth situations, without delving too deeply into psychological implications. They offer lighthearted and concise glimpses of everyday scenarios, encompassing both the ups and downs depending on how they appear in the spread, and which suit they share the space with. So there's no need to shuffle the cards to have them appear in both upright and reversed positions. You can simply shuffle them as you would for a game of poker, without reversing their orientation. As you know, this book isn't about a specific Tarot deck. The idea behind it is to give you the freedom to choose the one that resonates with you, without feeling obligated to start with a particular deck just because of its symbolism. My aim is to encourage you to put in the effort to imagine where you've already encountered or sensed the meaning of the Arcana and create your own personal reference guide based on your memories and experiences. However, I should mention that at the beginning it can be helpful to explore the Minor

Arcana of a Rider-Waite-Smith deck. These cards are illustrated with little scenes that partially capture the essence of each card, providing an extra hint for their interpretation. Think of them as the notes we used to sneak into our pencil cases before exams. They'll provide that extra support and guidance as you navigate the world of Tarot.

Now that you've grasped their essence, let me delve into how to interpret them, starting with their numbers and directing them based on their respective suits. Trust me, it's a much easier approach than memorizing the individual meanings of all 56 Arcana. Plus, you'll find it's a more effortless way to absorb their nuances, without having to clear up memory space on your brain's hard drive.

From 1 to 10: numerology for dummies

Although I never excelled in mathematical acumen at school, I have always been drawn to numbers and their constant presence in our existence. Numbers are literally everywhere and are one of the most powerful symbols that humanity has used. They identify, categorize, create sequences, measure quantities and distances, and give us the value of a certain thing. While they can define a beginning and an end (as happens in the Major Arcana), in their nature they are infinite and immeasurable, and that's why they are fascinating to me, being both precise and mysterious. Their form and what they represent create a positive or negative energetic response in humans. Have you ever heard someone say, "I don't want an appointment on the 13th because it's unlucky" or "I want the number 4 because I like it"? I believe you have!

In the Minor Arcana, we find the numbers from 1 to 10, known as Pythagorean numbers, named after the esteemed mathematician Pythagoras. Since numbers are symbols, each one carries a distinct meaning that can be positive or negative, receptive or active. This meaning is influenced by the number of the card that precedes or follows it.

Now, let me break it down for you in the simplest way possible, my dear Bae, so you can grasp the essence of each number and understand the fundamentals of every Minor Arcanum card.

ONE: In the Minor Arcana, this number is referred to as the Ace. It's the first number, and what does it bring to mind right away? Well, for me, it immediately evokes a sense of beginnings. Something starting, ready to blossom and grow. If you reflect on your early years, your first year of life, and the boundless potential and pathways that lay ahead, along with the progress you've made, it's easy to remember the essence of this number. One represents infinite possibilities. It's a planted seed that yields abundant fruits, a brilliant spark that ignites a fire, a hope, a thought that breathes life into matter. One signifies individualism. It's who we are before encountering doubt and change.

TWO: This is the number that brings One out of its lonesomeness. Here, we encounter unity, drawing closer to something (or someone) that shares our same vibration or with whom we may have disagreements. That's why it's always important to engage in dialogue, laying our ideas on the table alongside those of others, creating a path that leads us toward the other. Two represents the poles of a magnet, which, when they're opposites, come together, but when they're the same, repel each other. This number prompts us to collaborate, as it signifies the realm of our dearest friends and soulmates, but also of our opposites—teaching us to coexist. We haven't yet grasped the importance of shades and subtleties; here, everything is either black or white. The key lies in finding the formula to make them coexist or understanding how to manage the tension. Two embodies the spirit of duality and the binary.

THREE: "If before we were two, dancing the hully gully, now we are three, still grooving to the hully gully." We've added an extra member, as if the previous two had come together to create something new. Indeed, Three is the number of fertility and creation, bringing forth tangible outcomes. It's like the offspring of One and Two! It can also represent the resolution of tension that arose with number Two, or it can signify something entirely distinct. Think about mixing two colors: instead of blending into a shade of either, they create an entirely different tone, a fresh result. Or consider the saying, "When two quarrel, a third rejoices": the presence of a third party can bring harmony or decisively resolve the conflict with an unforeseen action. Three is about enrichment, adding a pinch of spice to an otherwise basic recipe.

FOUR: The square, and by extension the cube, is a geometric figure that, if turned around, remains unchanged. It doesn't alter its shape, always presenting sides that are equal to each other, evoking a sense of stability, steadfastness, and absolute predictability. Four symbolizes fulfillment, structure, and liberation from worries. On one hand, it brings us comfort because it's a truly dependable number, but on the other hand, too much consolidation can lead to boredom and a tendency to become complacent. For some, staying within their comfort zone is the ultimate life goal, but if we only solidify what we already possess or know, without venturing into new discoveries, we may find ourselves at ease but devoid of fresh inspiration. Four embodies rest and contemplation, while also nudging us to ponder what lies beyond our gilded boundaries.

FIVE: When I think of this number, it always brings to mind "V for Vendetta," representing the Roman numeral Five. You see, I have a special gift called synesthesia, where my brain associates multiple senses with a single stimulus. So, for instance, I "see" music and musical notes, and among other things, I tend to associate numbers and colors.When I think of number Five, I "see" it as a vibrant shade of red. It embodies action, but also carries the weight of violence and war. To me, it's a truly Martian number, instigating challenges and injecting an unexpected energy into the tranquil realm of number Four. Five disrupts the norm, testing our very foundations. It's like the loyal companion of the Hierophant card questioning his unwavering authority that has persisted through the ages. But don't let this number become your foe, for while it may ignite friction, it also sparks movement and transformation. That's why we must ask ourselves, how do we dance in the presence of this little earthquake, rather than solely fixating on the agent that triggers it? Five represents disruption and rebellion, shattering the monotony of an otherwise mundane silence.

SIX: With this number, we return to harmony, where we can create pairs once again. Everything is in order, balanced, and pleasing to the eye. Even its shape is super aesthetic—it resembles a comma, a little curl, adding a touch of charm to the simplicity and perfection of a circle. We're talking about the balance of Two combined with the stability of Four—a peace that arises from the harmonious nature of these two even numbers. Alternatively, it's the dual creativity brought forth by the double Three, leading to the long-awaited completion of the project initiated with this number. Six is the enjoyment of success, the celebration of a battle won after overcoming the many challenges presented by Five. We stand in front of the mirror, grooming and making ourselves look polished to receive our well-deserved prize and generously savor the fruits of our labor with a joyful spirit and open-heartedness.

SEVEN: This number is divided between the quest for independence and the need to form connections and communicate with the people we encounter along the journey of our lives. Your personal growth traverses a deeply spiritual path, often propelling you to explore what lies within. To embark on this inner journey, you will need to tread a path that leads you to discover realities and cultures different from your own. However, it is crucial to be wary of easy distractions and enticing temptations that may scatter your energies in futile pursuits. The potential is immense, but if you lose pieces of yourself along the way, the process of maturation may prove longer than anticipated. Seven can be likened to the wanderings of Odysseus seeking his way home, encountering the enchanting Sirens who represent his most tantalizing desires, passions, and the curiosity that beckons him to explore their alluring voices.

EIGHT: Cosmic balance and constant energy flow, Eight holds a place of profound reverence, as it embodies cycles and transformative changes that lead to spiritual elevation and transcendence to higher liminal realms. However, this cyclic nature can become a vicious circle if we fail to embrace movement. In its perfectly symmetrical form, it represents balance. When placed horizontally, it becomes the lemniscate, more commonly known as the infinity symbol, and it is the only number that remains the same when mirrored. With this number, I identify perfection, the embrace of multiple ideas, and a conclusion that unfailingly gives birth to new dawn.

NINE: I've always pictured this number as pure and moonlit, shining in pristine white. It embodies the realm of dreams and desires, with a visionary and idealistic nature that isn't necessarily a bad thing—quite the opposite! Remember, even utopia is a form of creative expression. Nine carries the infinite potential of all its preceding digits, so don't set limits on what you can or want to achieve. Your attitude can inspire other kindred souls to open up to you and join you on this incredible journey. You have the power to make a difference for the greater good, sharing the wisdom you've gained in the journey you've embarked on from One all the way here. Nine is all about sharing and spreading knowledge, about passing down the results of your successes, and narrating your personal truth to the world. But be cautious not to spread yourself too thin, conceding too much of your energy and attention to other people, as excessive focus on others can bring intense emotional stress that might make you falter. Stay true to yourself while making a positive impact.

TEN: It's the number of triumphs definitively accomplished, the grand finale of a massive show we have painstakingly prepared. Ten is like the thrilling last season of a series that has truly captivated us for months—or even years! It's the "happily ever after" type of conclusion, bidding farewell to an ending while embracing the knowledge that a fresh beginning awaits you around the corner. It comprises the essence of One, symbolizing beginnings, and the mystical Zero, representing rebirth in the vast realm of Chance. Yet, for all the excitement and anticipation of success, this jubilant milestone can weigh heavily on our shoulders, draining us of all remaining energies with the burden of high expectations. If we don't feel that we have achieved everything we aimed for, if this completion hasn't been shared with fellow travelers on our path, the accomplishment may feel bittersweet and hard-won.

The Four Suits

Well, now that we have explored a bit of numerology together, in the same simple way, I will try to explain to you what suits are, what their purpose is, and how they vary depending on the type. As you have already understood, the structure of the Minor Arcana is very similar to that of regular playing cards, so the concept of suits should be familiar to you.

In Tarot, each "seed" develops into 10 cards, along with the Court figures, which represent the full potential of each suit as they blossom and reach their peak. So, it's as if we're witnessing the growth of a planted seed from a tiny sprout to a magnificent tree. Each suit is associated with a natural element, providing additional insights into their characteristics and how they manifest in a reading, as well as their interactions with neighboring Arcana: water extinguishes fire, air fuels the flames of fire, water nurtures the earth, air stirs the waters, fire consumes the earth, and air sweeps across the land.

In a reading, just like in life, the ideal scenario is finding a balance among these elements. If one suit dominates over the others, it signifies that its corresponding element is taking precedence. So, by understanding the symbiotic relationship between the suits and their elemental associations, we gain deeper insights into the Tarot's wisdom and the dynamics at play within a reading.

The suits are Wands, Cups, Swords, and Pentacles (or Coins), and each of them adds a nuance to the number to help you understand which area of your life (or Ms. Betty's life) it influences. In the pages that follow, I'll explain each one to you. Ready? Let's go!

WANDS: They are usually represented as thick branches or wooden clubs. In the Marseille Tarot deck, they are depicted elegantly, contrary to their portrayal in the Napoletane or the Piacentine, where they appear as slightly crooked branches, resembling primitive cavemen's clubs. Do you remember Fred Flintstone, when he asked his wife Wilma to pass him the club? Well, it had the exact shape of the Wands we find on our cards. This suit represents the element of Fire, which activates our life force and makes us feel alive, powerful, and active. Wands symbolize creativity, the energy we harness when initiating something, and our willpower.

They speak to our sexual life, how we express our desires, cravings, ambitions for conquest, and all-around expansion. I don't like associating them too much with work and career because if a Wand card appears in a love reading, and like other authors, I were to tell you that this suit is related to work, you would feel confused and struggle to fit this meaning into an answer about emotions. So, focus instead on the fact that this is the suit of passion, will, strength (even physical), vigor, and courage. You will find that your interpretation flows more smoothly, and you won't be confused. An excess of Wands in a reading can bring tyranny, brute force that is absolutely unnecessary for the situation at hand, and a dispersal of energy without channeling it into something concrete. This is the suit that brings to mind sayings like "all smoke and no fire" or "barking dogs seldom bite." As I mentioned, I have an old soul and appreciate old sayings! Our goal for these branches is to make them flourish, to ensure they bear fruit. Sometimes, it may be necessary to use them as weapons, but without going overboard. It is better to unite them together to create a forest or a grove and witness them blossom in all their green wonder.

CUPS: Any container used to hold a liquid can be compared to a cup. When you wake up in the morning and drink your coffee or herbal tea, you use a cup to contain it. When you need to wash a sweater, you take a basin or put a plug the sink and fill it with water. Enclosing and containing is a fundamental action of a cup because it manages to delimit a liquid that, by its nature, is otherwise difficult to gather or control. As you may have understood, Cups are associated with the element of Water, with its fluidity and the ability to reflect, flow, and moisten. We can think of the sea, a stream, or a lake, but also tears, rain, and typhoons. This element can be as peaceful as it is destructive if it takes over, and the ability to contain it allows for analysis and positive utilization. What is more overflowing than emotions and feelings? It is precisely in these areas of our lives that this suit is concerned, as well as with receptivity (which always recalls the welcoming vessel represented by the Cup), dreams, artistic inspirations, and kindness. Just as the Water zodiac signs do, this suit invites us to explore the depths, fully immersing ourselves in our emotions. We must learn to swim without being overwhelmed by their intensity or deceived by their seemingly calm surface. It's a delicate balance of knowing when to ride the waves and when to simply float. Cups can offer us moments of exquisite pleasure, like indulging in a luxurious spa, or they can bring a sense of drowning and overwhelm. The key lies in the quantity and presence of Cup cards in a reading. An excess of Cups can turn receptiveness into passivity, love into overly sentimental drama, dreams into elusive illusions, and tears into an unending river, as Justin

Timberlake sang in "Cry Me a River." To evolve, it is crucial to gracefully navigate the ebb and flow of emotions, releasing any excess water that threatens to overflow, and finding a larger cup capable of holding our deepest feelings. This way, we can raise a toast to our joy and celebrate life's experiences.

SWORDS: During the Middle Ages and throughout the time when the practice of death penalty by decapitation was active, noble individuals had the privilege of receiving a well-executed and less painful beheading using a sword. The sword, being much sharper and precise than an axe, was reserved for nobles, while the axe was typically used for common criminals and ordinary people. With a single swift stroke, the sword swiftly severs heads, but it also cuts short conversations that linger for too long or situations that stagnate due to a lack of ideas. With this suit, we speak of quick thinking, intellect, sudden ideas that come at the right moment, our ability for verbal expression, and communication in general. The sword can protect but also inflict harm, and just like a blade, I am ready to unsheath of my beloved sayings: "Those who live by the sword, die by the sword," which perfectly encapsulates the essence of this suit. The meaning behind this phrase, found in the Gospel of Matthew, is that the use of violence (verbal or physical) generates more violence and thus more suffering. It is always better to calibrate the strength of our weapon, especially when it is so sharp. The Swords are associated with the element of Air, invisible yet capable of moving even the most solid individuals or situations, just as the wind shapes the form of cliffs. When used wisely, they enable us to analyze situations with great rationality and intelligence, guide us to speak the right words at the right time, urge us to study and enrich ourselves culturally, and help us organize our thoughts to find solutions to our problems. An excess of Swords leads to cutting wounds that are difficult to heal, to overthinking that confines us to live situations only in our mind without actively resolving them, to having a tongue sharper than a sword, and to an extremely vengeful and conflict-ridden social life. The balance of this suit is achieved when we know how to use our weapon to defend fairness, upholding the principles of noble justice, and heal from the wounds it can cause.

PENTACLES: "All the things I could do / if I had a little money / it's a rich man's world," sang ABBA in *Money, Money, Money*. Indeed, the energy of money carries the potential for self-realization, serving as the literal currency that values our actions economically, enabling our sustenance and, why not, comfort. In the depictions of the Rider-Waite-Smith deck, this suit is illustrated as a coin with the design of a pentacle, the name by which this suit is referred to. The symbol of the five-pointed star, when upright, represents mankind's dominion over the four elements. This suit is linked to the Earth element and the realm of the material, encompassing all that is tangible. It's the strong bond between humanity's mastery over the elements and the tangible nature of coins. They represent the attainment of material stability, where tradition solidifies, overshadowing the uncertainty of the avant-garde, just like the Hierophant and the Devil, the two cards most rooted in Earth among all the Major Arcana. If we observe the structure of these two cards in their traditional depictions, we can see a figure with outstretched arms, towering over the two disciples in the Hierophant and the two demons in the Devil. If we place a point at each end of the illustration, we have one at the head, two for the arms, and two for each disciple/demon. Five points that, when connected, form the shape of a Pentacle! This suit encompasses the drive to attain and relish accumulated wealth, while also encompassing the persistent discontent that arises when these objectives remain unfulfilled. Additionally, it cautions against the complacency that can ensue from excessive comfort, risking stagnation and inertia. If we indulge excessively, we become as greedy as Scrooge: swimming in gold may seem fun, but its weight can crush and dominate us, leaving us emotionally and generously impoverished. And let's remember, to offer a fitting maxim here as well, "All that glitters is not gold!" Great wealth may be tempting, but it also has its negative aspects. Sometimes it's better to have less but learn to appreciate it. This is precisely the balance of the Pentacles: finding material satisfaction while also learning to share it without forgetting the emotions it brings us.

Court gossip: who are the Page, Knight, Queen, and King?

The path that starts from number One, the Ace, and takes us to fulfillment in number Ten is like a grand avenue leading us to the Court, where we can put into practice everything we have learned, reaching our highest potential. It's time for a proper introduction to the residents of this imaginary castle, one by one, as we explore the four Court figures, each belonging to their respective suits. Let the trumpets sound and the drums roll! Dress your best, I must say, for soon you will be in the presence of nobility!

THE PAGE: This character can come to you with different names: Page, Knave, Jack, or even Lady in some decks. They're going through that post-high school phase, fully immersed in their adolescence, with the acne, love at first sight, and the excitement that defines this stage of life. Fueled by good intentions, they're also flawed due to their lack of experience. Does it ring a bell? It kind of reminds me of the energy of the Magician, with their untapped potential and eagerness to dive in, but also with their impatience and naivety, trying their best to appear credible. From this figure, we can definitely learn about freshness, evoking the drive we had at eighteen, the thirst for the world and knowledge that pushes us to take initiative in the face of opportunities, and the inherent ability to learn during adolescence. It's like going back to the school desks in spirit, while still being aware that, unfortunately or fortunately, there are few responsibilities at that age. Let's embrace the super-youthful attitude as a positive attribute, rather than as a means to evade obligations. The Page is associated with the Earth element.

THE KNIGHT: After completing their apprenticeship, the Page hops on a horse and, with gusto or maybe a bit of recklessness, becomes the messenger, delivering missives left and right. They're basically the Tarot's very own Pony Express, trotting around with important news. This figure brings to mind Atreyu from *The Neverending Story*, riding his faithful steed Artax (some folks still get teary-eyed thinking about the Swamps of Sadness). Or imagine them soaring through the sky on the back of a Luck Dragon, bravely striving to save the kingdom of Fantasia from the encroaching The Nothing, untangling a situation that seemed doomed. The fact that they're on a noble steed signifies movement, urging you to take an active leap to resolve a situation or stir up the waters, to seize what the Page has learned in theory and spread the word throughout the realm about the purpose of your mission. The Knight's dynamic energy is like the vibrant brushstrokes found in Futurist artworks. Have you ever seen Umberto Boccioni's masterpiece *The City Rises*? It's worth a look to grasp the essence and character embodied by this figure. The Knight is closely connected to the element of Air.

THE QUEEN: This figure instantly brings to mind the Mothers of the Ball Culture, the vibrant birthplace of voguing—a dance form that emerged in the 1980s in the United States, serving as an expression of feeling out of place in a society where white, straight privilege reigns supreme, leaving marginalized communities like Black, Hispanic, LGBTQ+, and transgender individuals on the fringes. But let me tell you, it's not just about the dance moves—it's a whole world. In the Ball Culture, every group of dancers forms their own "house," replacing the families they may have been separated from due to their gender or sexual orientation. And who leads these houses? The Mothers, of course! They take care of the communal living spaces, provide guidance and support to their adopted "Kids," and embody loyalty, resilience, and an unyielding love for both the art of dance and the people they embrace as their chosen family. Thanks to these Mothers, the Kids have the opportunity to find their place in the world and have a second chance to achieve fulfillment through artistic expression. Sharing and generosity are ingrained in the very essence of the houses. Now, let's talk about the Queen, one of the Court figures. She embodies a nurturing sanctuary, a source of nourishment and care. She represents the gestation period before an idea becomes tangible or communication takes shape. The Queen guides us in processing our emotions and finding the perfect outlet to let them flow. She imparts a sense of noble character and deep wisdom, serving as both a confidant and a trusted advisor. In times of need, she's the kind of friend we all yearn for. The Queen is intimately connected to the element of Water.

THE KING: Finally, the long-awaited completeness and maturity have arrived. It's safe to say that we can't go much higher, although, of course, there is always room for improvement if desired. The King has been tested many times, and both victory and defeat have shaped him into a confident individual. He is not flawless or fearless, but his sense of security keeps him focused, utilizing his full potential, especially when faced with challenging battles. Having experienced all the previous stages, the Queen stands by his side, encouraging him to reflect on the emotional aspects that, due to his outward drive, he sometimes tends to overlook. His subjects are also his offspring, whom he educates and shapes within the realms represented by each suit, earning their respect while simultaneously creating future Kings by instilling in them confidence, a passion for life, the sense of seeking their own stability, and the importance of making their voices heard. This figure doesn't need to insist on being in command of something; his aura and reputation precede him. It's exactly the kind of vibe we need to emanate when we work on our self-worth and the boundaries that those around us are expected to respect, showcasing our tangible achievements with pride. However, we must always be mindful of excesses and not become arrogant know-it-alls, as it's easy to succumb to the flattery of compliments and transform into the most conceited and unbearable version of a ruler. The King also embodies a proud posture, so stand tall when the time comes for your coronation. Go, Bae, break through and conquer the world! Of course, the King is associated with the element of Fire.

ACE OF WANDS

THE ACES · The spark

ACE OF WANDS: This marvelous, gnarled baseball bat appears before us as an unexpectedly helpful tool to shake up our lives. Bae, you know that feeling when you're bored to death and suddenly the urge to clean the entire house or go out and party hits you? That's your Ace of Wands. This is the card that anyone working with creativity would love to see, as it sparks ideas on how to give your project a boost or start a new one, showcasing your evocative power in bringing something to life. With this Arcanum, my advice is to go for it! Come on! You just need to keep that spark alive and determine if it holds potential or if it's just a flash in the pan. What happens around the Wand? Is there water to extinguish it? Or is there air blowing upon it, intensifying its flames? Reflect on the power of the elements: if the fire becomes overwhelming and lacks a guiding element, be prepared to call the firefighters.

ACE OF CUPS: Are you thirsty for emotions? Is your life feeling dry? Here comes just the thing that will quench your thirst—a Jacuzzi of emotions and affection to immerse yourself in while sipping on a margarita or a glass of bubbly! Listen to the rhythm of your heart and unlock it as if you were a hippie in San Francisco during the Summer of Love. The level of engagement in whatever you're facing is intense, no matter the context. It's like falling in love for the first time, or that rush you get when you see the ocean. So let every fiber of your being soak in this sensation without any barriers. But hey, we need to be careful about what surrounds this Cup: Is the road wide open or is there a roadblock? What's diverting our stream? Are we absolutely sure we're not overdoing it by opening this dam? If downstream there isn't a big enough basin to contain us, then flood alarms are ringing! Even the most skilled swimmer risks drowning if there's too much water and nothing to channel it or a solid anchor to hold on to.

ACE OF SWORDS: Here you go, Bae, a more refined weapon to embark on your new journey. Take this elegant saber and feel the swishes it sings with every graceful swing. With every strike, envision unleashing a brilliant idea or uttering the perfect word at the precise moment. It's evident that with your intellect, you have the potential to become someone truly significant, thanks to your fairness and skill in balancing judgments and resolving conflicts. But beware: if you're not the sole sword in the deck, you may find yourself in a position where defense becomes necessary. Our blade's mastery becomes fierce, as if engaged in a duel. Remember, your weapon is still in its elemental stage and could inadvertently sever heads that should not be touched or succumb to reckless frenzy. So, don't dwell too long on what could become a futile display. What else lies within your spread? Is it Water, cleansing your blade? Is it Fire, fueling its passion? Or is it Earth, bringing a sense of calm?

ACE OF PENTACLES: The coin that Super Mario collects in every level, gradually building his treasure, or Scrooge McDuck's Number One Dime that sparked his vast fortune—we all started with a lone piece of gold to learn the worth of material things and their significance. Being present, inhabiting our bodies, embracing the moment not as a fleeting instant but as a chapter in which we can already lay the foundation for our future—these are all themes woven into this Arcanum. In this Ace, even the tiniest seed carries meaning when seen through the lens of perspective. No sequoia was born majestic; it, too, started as a tiny seedling. The essence of giving ourselves, whether it's our abilities or resources, lies in helping something small become something great. Look around: How significant is this little coin? Is it our winning investment, or are we giving it too much value? Is it being nourished or is it being buried?

A PLAYLIST FOR THE ACES

When a Fire Starts to Burn—Disclosure

Begin Again—Purity Ring

Wanna Be Startin' Somethin'—Michael Jackson

Sowing the Seeds of Love—Tears for Fears

Still in doubt?
Consider how the four suits can be applied to the Magician.

TWO OF SWORDS

TWO · You and I

TWO OF WANDS: If this Arcanum appears and there's an opportunity to merge one's idea with someone else's, let's go for it! The key is to be aligned in having constructive and similar intentions; otherwise, brace yourselves for a clash. That's why dialogue is crucial, aiming in the same direction, to avoid throwing a spanner in each other's works. Mutual respect is paramount. The Two of Wands represents the power of one flame meeting another to burn with greater intensity, not a competition to outshine one another. If we've planned to launch our project initiated by the Ace, have we considered the additional possibilities that may arise if we meet someone who burns with the same intensity along the way? There's a sappy quote I could add to this card to give you some insight: "Love does not consist of gazing at each other, but in looking outward together in the same direction" (as written by Antoine de Saint-Exupéry, the author of *The Little Prince*). When the two Wands unite, do they do so for a common purpose or to overpower one another?

TWO OF CUPS: Cheers! This is a true toast to our health! We recognize each other as kindred spirits and speak the same emotional language. A bit of our essence flows into the other's cup and vice versa. But wait, where have we seen two cups before, if we're using a traditional deck? In Temperance: the angelic figure continuously pours the liquid between two vessels, embodying harmony and tranquility, while the woman in the Star Arcanum pours water from her two vessels to revitalize the stream at her feet. In both cases, water represents life and healing. In the Two of Cups, it also serves as the bond between two individuals who have found each other and seal their encounter with a drink (you know, when two people intertwine arms when toasting) Now, take a look at how the surrounding Arcana behave: Is there a sword attempting to sever this union? Or money being drenched with a double dose of water? Is there a fire burning in the log burner as we draw closer, gazing into each other's eyes? Or do our emotions help temper the ardor that might otherwise flare up excessively?

TWO OF SWORDS: Here, we can engage in a spirited duel, which can also lead to a thought-provoking confrontation. You see, back in the Middle Ages, the term "tenso" referred to a lively exchange of ideas in academic circles. Over time, it came to encompass the concept of dueling to defend one's honor. So, let me invite you to ponder this point: when you protect your ideas, is it merely a matter of taking a stance, or does it also reflect who you are and what you truly believe in? A conflict can bring about reconciliation, but it can also result in irreparable damage. When two swords are locked in combat, they form a pair of shears, and their cut becomes difficult to heal. Is it truly worth it? Take a moment to reflect and decide whether to proceed or find a way to open yourself up to new ideas, fresh perspectives, and alternative ways of thinking. If the two swords cross each other, they create an X, a formidable barrier. What are you blocking? Are you avoiding compromise or standing in the way of a situation that requires dialogue? Consequently, are you overlooking the multitude of possible resolutions that your mind is capable of generating? Take the time to meditate on these thoughts and determine whether you want to clash swords or gracefully open your blades as a symbol of welcoming access to your world.

TWO OF PENTACLES: To find stability, we must embrace change. What we possess, our very core, shifts to accommodate what comes from the outside. In our wallet, we make space for a new coin. Matter transforms to generate greater wealth. It's like when we transform our living spaces, making adjustments for a new roommate or partner, combining our strengths and resources. This Arcanum also makes us reflect on how we invest our precious resources. Do we do it wisely, or do we sometimes go a little overboard, filling up our online shopping carts with things that we'll soon regret clicking "buy now" on? And when we extend a helping hand to others, do we remember to keep something for ourselves? It's essential to examine how we feel when we have a little extra. Do we generously offer a drink to anyone we encounter, or do we quietly keep it to ourselves?

A PLAYLIST FOR TWOS
2 Become 1—Spice Girls
Sweet Harmony—The Beloved

SONGS FROM ITALY
Fuoco nel Fuoco—Eros Ramazzotti
Due—Raf

Still in doubt?
Consider how the four suits can be applied to the High Priestess.

195

THREE OF WANDS

THREE · Ctrl+C/Ctrl+V

THREE OF WANDS: Let's throw another log onto the previous two and watch our fire transform that mere spark from the Ace into something remarkable. There's boundless creativity and the tangible manifestation of something truly explosive, thanks to the harmonious interplay of the two Wands we encountered earlier. When this card appears in a reading, it's a call to team up with someone and realize that together, we have the power to accomplish extraordinary feats. This Arcanum beckons us to embrace adventure. Have you ever considered checking out those last-minute flights? Beyond your usual circle, you might stumble upon enriching experiences that add fascinating new dimensions to your life. I really love this Arcanum because it positively enhances both our personal and professional relationships. It's like a sprinkle of magic, with an exhilarating effect. The Three of Wands makes us feel like we can conquer the world, it fuels our audacity and leaves us hungry for exploration, eager to bring to life what we could only dream of before. However, it's important to know if we are setting unrealistic or actually achievable goals, or else energy drain is just around the corner. Think of the explosive trio of the 2000s, Paris Hilton, Britney Spears, and Lindsay Lohan: individually, their creative potential could have been incredible, but when united, they generated a fiery, almost destructive energy, yet undeniably iconic.

THREE OF CUPS: A card that speaks of the power of friendship and the overwhelming affection you feel when you meet your soulmates and you're so happy that you want to throw a party just to shout it to everyone. You feel closely connected to the sensation of finally being understood and supported for who you are and what you feel, and it's a fulfilling feeling. In the realm of work or projects, what you create is validated and recognized, and you feel capable of giving even more without feeling the burden, but rather realizing that your performance is through the roof. The desire to go out and proclaim it to the world is incredibly strong, so go ahead and do it! Put on your most stylish party outfit, make a drinks list, and go have fun, but not before calling the people who are most like you and with whom you share a deep bond. Your emotions are in harmony with the surrounding environment, and everything around you is fluid and smooth. This is the perfect blend of seemingly different elements that coexist in mutual respect and complete fusion. In my opinion, this card can also be associated with gender fluidity. In the Three of

Cups, the only potential risk, if the surrounding cards are very stagnant, is that of excessive indulgence. It's like when you're at a great party and you don't want to leave, being nearly addicted to fun and pleasure.

THREE OF SWORDS: When the Empress has her heart broken, this card proceeds to manifest itself. How many times has it happened in your life that you had to part ways with something or someone you cared about, especially if you weren't the one to choose this separation? Remember that breakups also serve to grow and understand that not everything is permanent in our lives. Swords are a suit associated with intellect, so the more this separation works on how we tend to idealize a person, a relationship, a job, or a thought, the stronger the desire for revenge will be. Because when something breaks, we feel as if a bolt of lightning has struck us, revealing the reality of the situation, and shattering the idyllic dream we had been nurturing until then. The advice is not to refuse to see things as they truly are, not to try to piece together the fragments that connect us to what has been destroyed, but rather to see this opportunity as a way to heal our wounded hearts. This card reminds me of the Japanese technique of Kintsugi: when a ceramic object breaks, its pieces are repaired using gold, transforming it into something new and beautiful that proudly displays its scars. Its breakage does not signify its end but a new beginning, thanks to the process of healing.

THREE OF PENTACLES: Once the break is over, it's time to get back to work. The satisfaction of being able to see and enjoy the fruits of our labor is the well-deserved compensation for our dedicated efforts. It's about choosing to work diligently and seeking the engagement and support of like-minded individuals who share the same goals. In various areas of inquiry, this is the card of team building, the ability to work as a team without dominance or power plays. How do you relate to others when it's time to join forces? Do you thrive in a group, or do you seek to stand out from others, wanting the spotlight of success solely on yourself? Reflect on the importance of having support. If you feel stronger in the company of others, make the most of the ability to work together with other people to reach your goal in less time, and perhaps with collective attention to detail. If you are still at the stage where learning together is key, I discourage individual endeavors due to limited experience. Learning to observe how people around you move and interact, driven by the desire to achieve a common goal, will teach you a lot about yourself as well. Look at the surrounding cards: Are there any Swords? Who is trying to sabotage this cooperation? Is it other people, yourself, or the misaligned intentions of the members of this group?

Still in doubt?
Consider how the four suits can be applied to the Empress.

FOUR OF PENTACLES

FOUR · I am just fine

FOUR OF WANDS: What have you accomplished in your previous battles and creative endeavors? Have you earned respect, or perhaps something more tangible? And mind you, respect is certainly something tangible. It's always gratifying to be appreciated by someone. You've brought home the results, marking the crucial first step in the hero's journey, that moment when you mistakenly believe (because the road ahead is still long) that you've achieved something significant. And so, you eagerly share your excitement, daydreaming about collapsing onto the couch after a joyous celebration. Of course, a bit of rest is well-deserved, reaching out to a friend to share the good news and raising a glass together. But beware of prematurely singing victory and succumbing to post-triumph laziness halfway through the journey. If the surrounding cards depict passivity (an excessive number of Pentacles or Cups), you might feel the pull of complacency as you've reached one-third of your intended goal. The temporary stability achieved can easily lead to taking it all for granted, no longer fighting for progress. So set aside the popcorn, kick off those slippers, for there are more adventures to be embarked upon if you truly seek lasting security.

FOUR OF CUPS: This card is all about the contentment of those who aspire to "settle down" in life, in every aspect. They meet someone or take on a job that may not even excite them all that much, but they give off this sense of being secure, just like that, without questioning themselves anymore. It's like playing a card game of blackjack: you don't know the dealer's hand, but you settle because you don't want to take any risks. You'd rather stay in the middle, without asking for more cards. The problem is that life could offer you so much more (and I'm not just talking about card games, of course), but you choose to stay where you are, ignoring the opportunities that come your way, because you have no intention of stepping out of your comfort zone and challenging your secure spots, especially the emotional ones. With other passive cards or ones that signal some sort of annoyance, it's like listening to a Radiohead song when you're already feeling sleepy or down: it's like a hammer hitting your head, keeping you tucked away in your own little corner while life goes on outside. The lesson of this card is that you need to wake up from the drowsiness of a life that's too bland. The world is brimming with exciting opportunities that can turn your life around for the better, and you might end up regretting not seizing them when they literally came knocking at your door.

FOUR OF SWORDS: If you've made wise choices with the Ace, the Four wants to tell you that now is the time to contemplate and let them mature, or perhaps put them into action later. Pay attention to the shape your thoughts take as you rest or reflect, allowing them to flow freely. If you've used words poorly, this card advises you to accept it without adding anything more. It's not the moment to exert yourself trying to patch up something that was said with too much force or in a misguided manner. Allow everything in your intellectual sphere to settle. This card is perfect for a Bae who tends to overthink and exhaust their mind, as it encourages you to contemplate without burning out your synapses. Consider embarking on a meditation journey or embracing the practice of silence. Take breaks from your thoughts and use this time to find inner clarity. If there's an excess of Swords, it may feel like every mental input resonates in your head like a hammer on a gong, making it difficult to think clearly and react appropriately to events you may not be ready to face just yet.

FOUR OF PENTACLES: After successfully creating something, are you really going to hold back from showing off a bit of what you've achieved with the fruits of your labor? This card represents those who, after becoming prosperous (not without putting in a lot of hard work, of course), go ahead and buy an amazing car or dress from head to toe in designer labels. It's totally understandable to want to flaunt the results of your efforts from the Ace to the Three. But the question is, do you want your display to also convey a sense of superiority, power, and control over your life, just to prove to others that you've "made it"? How do you share your sense of accomplishment and the strength you've gained from it? Do you engage in philanthropy? Do you offer your skills to help others? Do you inspire someone? Or have you simply taken a seat on your throne, with an underlying fear that something might challenge you? The danger of this card is that you might become so enamored with your newfound stability that you risk becoming obsessed with it, constantly accumulating without ever feeling truly satisfied. If the surrounding cards lean toward passivity, you may find yourself lingering in this kind of behavior. On the other hand, if Swords dominate the spread, you're ready to fiercely defend your treasure or even fight to snatch away what belongs to others. Often, behind such prematurely achieved success, there are hidden vulnerabilities from the past that we try to compensate for with fame or material possessions. But if we learn to continuously question ourselves, we can truly embrace the tools necessary to enjoy the fulfillment of our goals without the constant fear of losing them overnight.

Still in doubt?

Consider how the four suits can be applied to the Emperor.

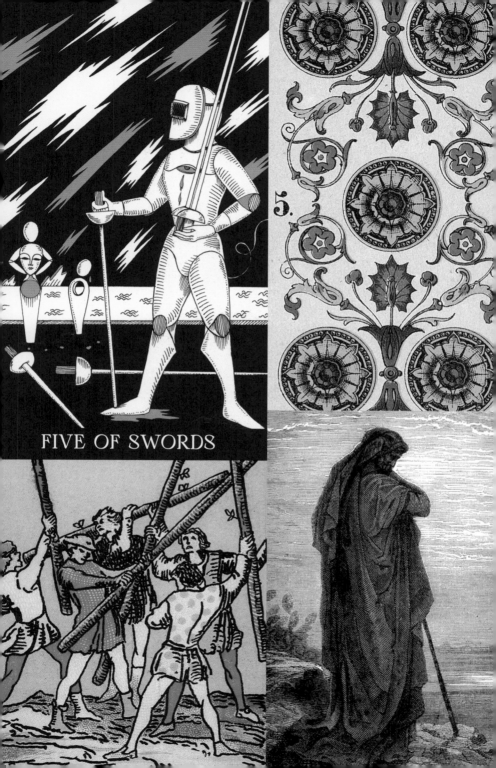

FIVE OF SWORDS

FIVE · Break free
from stability

FIVE OF WANDS: When your mind opens up to new opinions, how do you handle them? Do you find yourself caught between tradition and innovation, or do you see it as an opportunity to enrich what you've always considered a solid foundation? The pull is quite strong: on one hand, there's the fear of disrupting the harmony that defines our existence, but on the other hand, there's a nudge urging us to dive into the fray, expressing all the fresh ideas that come to mind. It could be a desire for a complete makeover, a yearning to try something completely new, or even taking a front seat in a discussion instead of staying in the background to preserve tranquility. How do you perceive the people involved in this situation—are they adversaries or potential allies? Can you find a middle ground, or perhaps, for a change, embrace the thrill of going against the grain and creating constructive friction? If accompanied by Swords cards, be cautious not to become an inconvenience for the sake of argument or to stoke the fires of tension that could be resolved differently. Otherwise, be prepared for a battle that may lead to a less honorable victory. This card brings to mind those who exploit conflicts for the sheer pleasure of chaos, without defending any particular ideals.

FIVE OF CUPS: After the revelry of Four, Five represents the emptiness that can linger after you've had your fill and must deal with the aftermath of emotions created by the abundance and pleasure experienced at that gathering. A sense of emptiness and melancholy grips you, and all that remains are scattered glasses, a headache, and the longing to recreate that sense of communion with others. If you've left a job or been let go, you focus solely on what has been lost rather than actively finding ways to fill that void. This card breeds dissatisfaction, but if not accompanied by suitable cards, we try to fill that void with temporary substitutes without truly mending it. Don't cry over spilled milk but reflect on the situation without identifying too strongly with the pain caused by the disruption of a previously fulfilling sentiment. If you believe that regret will simply fade away on its own, then you'll continue to gaze at your living room filled with remnants of the long-finished party for a while. If you've clung to the notion that the glass could always be half full simply because you assumed it was, then it would be wise to reconsider what emotional completeness means to you: whether it entails freezing things forever in a particular state or actively working to seek personal balance.

FIVE OF SWORDS: This card has an unpleasant vibe, to be honest. It urges us to delve into the individuals involved in a situation where honesty has been cast aside. The whole dynamic is far from crystal clear, and someone is taking advantage of the chaos to deceive and seek revenge. They wield the power of words like an iron fist, aiming to strike down a confused or wounded opponent. Picture yourself in a heated argument with someone you're not particularly fond of or someone who has wronged you in the past. Now imagine seeing them engaged in a fierce debate or being cornered by another interlocutor, their words leaving them vulnerable. What would you do in that moment? Would you relish the opportunity to retaliate and indulge in personal satisfaction, using the sharpest, most cutting words at your disposal? Or would you choose the path of peace, reflecting on the fact that revenge isn't always the right way to go? Remember, words carry tremendous weight— they can either caress or cut deep. Are you able to live with a clear conscience, accepting the consequences of your actions? Can you still claim to have a strong moral compass, or will the haunting feeling of having claimed a victim linger in your future?

FIVE OF PENTACLES: When you find yourself facing a problem, when your anchor points shift and seem to vanish, are you able to reach out to the people within your trusted circle for a helping hand, or do you reject their assistance? It often depends on the kind of support others offer you. Sometimes, hands are extended toward us, but we hesitate to grasp them—either because we fail to notice them or because accepting help would mean admitting that we have a problem, and we are unwilling to compromise with those who want to lend a hand. Bae, be mindful of this card and what follows, as the danger of believing that you're alone often stems from not acknowledging the network that stands ready to catch you and prevent your fall. It's like a wounded dog that bites the hand trying to soothe it. Don't conceal your loss—embrace the refuge being offered to you.

Still in doubt?
Consider how the four suits can be applied to the Hierophant.

SIX OF PENTACLES

SIX · Ridiculously handsome

SIX OF WANDS: We decided to jump right into the mix, partly for the thrill and partly because we were stubborn, and guess what? We came out victorious. Our choice to disrupt the stability paid off, and now we're being carried on people's shoulders like true stars. We have the power to influence others with our triumph, and our every move from here on out doesn't go unnoticed. The fire that ignited our ambitions for a life different from the one fate seemed to have laid out has also sparked a devoted following who openly praise us for our remarkable feats. What we've accomplished has gone viral, like when we record an awe-inspiring video, and it gets shared by countless viewers. We took a leap of faith, no doubt, but now is not the time to rest on our laurels, lest we come across as conceited, which serves no constructive purpose. We must stay consistent and not get blinded by the dazzling lights of fame. Otherwise, the lack of consistency in our work could turn the tables and paint us as fallen stars. Think about famous individuals who, caught up in their golden moments, let fame go to their heads, only to end up splashed across scandalous tabloids, squandering all the hard work that led them to their lofty heights.

SIX OF CUPS: Dear Bae, how often do you give yourself the chance to truly experience a deep and overwhelming emotion, like being moved to tears by something that deeply touches your heart or rediscovering the beauty in the simplest things? It could be a heartfelt gesture from someone, the realization of waking up and feeling content and secure, or recognizing that even in solitude, you have yourself and choose to embrace self-love. You can also allow yourself to momentarily retreat into cherished memories, triggered by a scent or engaging in a conversation with someone about those moments when you both felt truly alive. But it's important not to get trapped in a past that no longer exists. Use these memories as a catalyst to create new ones together and to live in the present without falling into the trap of overly romanticizing the past. How can you create a comforting environment around you, where the people you hold dear, including yourself, can feel safe to trust and freely express their emotions, fostering a reciprocal exchange that avoids triggering unpleasant memories? Consider how you can actualize this aspiration in your personal life, work, and any aspect of your life that relates to this card's message.

SIX OF SWORDS: I felt a strong connection to this Arcanum during a period of my life when what I had in my hometown had left me feeling dry, heartbroken, and exhausted to the point that, suddenly, I decided to embark on a journey to a nation 2,600 kilometers away from my hometown. I had the desire to rediscover myself, experience and explore new horizons. Bae, I invite you not to settle where there is nothing left for you, but to choose to invest your energy on an intellectual level by studying, traveling, and expanding your knowledge. You can decide to stay where everything feels familiar but limiting, or you can take a new direction that leads you on a journey where you can unleash your full potential. By doing so, you can overcome past disappointments or intrusive thoughts that once told you that you would never make it. The Erasmus experience is a good comparison to the Six of Swords: we acquire new knowledge by studying and living in a new place, opening ourselves up to the beauty of learning to connect with people different from ourselves.

SIX OF PENTACLES: Engaging in acts of charity is an incredibly noble deed because it helps individuals in need get the tools to lift themselves out of a crisis. It also extends to supporting marginalized groups, providing them with financial or moral support to pursue autonomy from those who exploit them. This applies not only to financial aid but also to acts of assistance in general. After all, money is an energy that passes from one person to another with the aim of helping those who are lacking or completely without it. This card, when driven by genuine intentions, tells you that it's time to give or accept the generosity that arises within the context of the question at hand. Think of the Five—if you were able to grasp it before, this is where that gesture comes to fruition, creating a situation of upliftment that allows you to appreciate the beauty of restored balance thanks to external intervention. But what's the surrounding context? Altruism isn't always spontaneous, and help can also be driven by self-interest. When you do someone a favor, do you do it spontaneously or do you expect the other person to sing your praises or repay you in the future? Sometimes, we employ benevolence as a strategy to feel superior to others or to seek public validation of our goodness and talent. However, this reveals a significant amount of hypocrisy that I encourage you to reflect upon, whether you find yourself on the receiving end or the one extending the helping hand.

Still in doubt?
Consider how the four suits can be applied to the Lovers.

SEVEN OF CUPS

SEVEN · Beyond frontiers

SEVEN OF WANDS: When it comes to this Arcanum, we delve into our inclination, or that of the querent, to handle debates or discussions with someone who holds a different view or brings forth a contrasting argument. Let me pose a question: When you engage in a conversation about something you deeply care about or have extensive knowledge of, and the person in front of you strongly disagrees, do you ignite with passion and vigorously defend your own ideas? Do you hurriedly turn to Google in search of supporting evidence for your thesis? Well, I must admit, I do! (Thanks to my Sagittarius ascendant.) The alternative is to embrace a dissenting voice or one that stands in direct opposition to what you have always held as true. Rather than perceiving it as a personal attack, consider it an opportunity to embrace a fresh perspective, without feeling compelled to adopt it as your own. This Seven is all about political debates, but it also represents the relentless pursuit of being right, even when even Google tells us that what we've long held on to is false or different from what we thought. How far are we willing to go to fight for a cause that seems so essential to us? How much do we personally identify with these battles? This card allows us to assert our autonomy by choosing what we stand for, but sometimes it wouldn't hurt to step down from our self-appointed pedestal, especially when we find ourselves both the speaker and the listener, with no one left to rally behind our words.

SEVEN OF CUPS: Who hasn't woken up from a dream thinking it was reality? Come on, raise your hand. I bet it's happened to all of us at least once in our lives. Every now and then, I have these ridiculously indulgent dreams where I go on a shopping spree for a super high-end designer bag or loads of brand-new, mind-blowing makeup in colors that only exist in the depths of my imagination. I wake up with this intense feeling that what I bought is real, only to be hit with disappointment when I realize it's all just a fantasy. But then, in the real world, I snap back to my senses and realize that those are nothing but frivolous objects, things I don't actually need at all, and the dissatisfaction fades away. The issue arises when the opposite occurs—when you're wide awake and your mind envisions you as the central figure in situations and triumphs that you have yet to experience or even make progress toward. Rather than succumbing to these visions, harness your imaginative capacity to define your objective, but remember to put in the hard work to attain it. Additionally, take the time to discern whether you're yearning for an illusion, something frivolous, or if there is a genuine necessity for you to possess that coveted object. Do you really want to be with that person, or is it just a matter of getting back at them or sticking to your principles? Is the growth you want to achieve driven by a desire for external validation or is it something you truly seek for yourself? The key here is the significance we give to our dreams: do we let ourselves be consumed by them or are we like our own fairy godmother, pushing ourselves in a positive way to make them come true? This Arcanum also reminds us of an important idea: do not be fooled by appearances.

SEVEN OF SWORDS: I must admit, I'm quite fond of this Arcanum, even though it doesn't always have a positive outlook. It embodies the ability to bring to life a wildly imaginative idea by carefully assessing the situation at hand, ensuring we emerge unscathed and get away with it in a given scenario. However, we must tread cautiously with the subsequent cards, as they will reveal whether we end up outsmarting others or falling victim to our own game. Nevertheless, if we find ourselves needing to seize the moment to secure victory in a dynamic where we aren't the sole protagonist, this card becomes paramount, urging us to employ our cleverness to tip the scales in our favor. For once, venturing beyond the ordinary can lead to a rewarding breakthrough. This card reminds me of the captivating tale of Chichibio and the Crane from Boccaccio's renowned work, the *Decameron*. Picture this scene: Chichibio, a talented chef, prepares an exquisite crane for his master's feast. However, just as he is about to present the dish, along comes Brunella, Chichibio's sweetheart, who requests a roasted leg with an implied threat to abandon him if her desire is not fulfilled. Being somewhat submissive, Chichibio willingly surrenders the desired leg to her. But here's the twist—when the dish is laid on the table, Currado, Chichibio's master, keenly observes that the bird is missing one of its legs. The cook then tries to convince the master that cranes only have one leg, and shows some of the same birds resting outside as proof. But Currado is not that gullible: he shouts to frighten the cranes and they all fly away, revealig the second leg. Chichibio's lie has been exposed, but instead of retracting he decides to joke about the episode saying that, had the master shouted to the roasted crane, that too would have showed him his other leg. If it fails to make you laugh, Bae, I remind you that the *Decameron* was written in the 14th century. Anyway, the essence of this card is that ingenuity is rewarded but beware of the surrounding cards: we might fall into arrogance, thinking we're the masters of deception, only to end up in an uncomfortable situation.

SEVEN OF PENTACLES: Here we have the card of the workaholic, someone who lives and swears by his work, putting in every ounce of effort to improve their situation and potentially reach a higher status than where they started. It's certainly a commendable endeavor, especially because in this Arcanum we see proof that the hard work put into the previous six Pentacles is paying off. Patience is rewarded, but it's also important to recognize that some results come naturally, without having to constantly sweat and toil. What does this mean? Well, sometimes, if we push ourselves too hard with relentless perseverance (and this can happen in a spread dominated by Pentacles), we risk losing ourselves in the pursuit of our desires, striving for an outcome that could have been achieved even if we had taken a gentler approach and savored the path that led us here. Despite the cautionary message carried by this Arcanum, the rewards of our efforts can extend to the inner work we undertake, especially if someone has pointed out our immaturity in the past or if we have made a conscious decision to become a better person. Such endeavors are truly praiseworthy. Just remember, from time to time, to assess the direction you're headed and the environment you're immersed in. Perhaps you've chosen to go into therapy, or the person you're reading the Tarot for has taken that path, or maybe you're investing your hard-earned money into something close to your heart, or you're striving for consistency in a particular endeavor. The key is not to lose sight of what truly matters to you and not to ignore the signals your body or mind send you, saying, "Rest" or "Enjoy what you have accomplished so far."

A PLAYLIST FOR SEVENS
Sweet Dreams (Are Made of This)—Eurythmics
Applause—Lady Gaga
Leave (Get Out)—JoJo
She Works Hard for the Money—Donna Summer

Still in doubt?
Consider how the four suits can be applied to the Chariot.

EIGHT OF WANDS

EIGHT · Practice
makes perfect

EIGHT OF WANDS: If this card made a sound, it would go swishhh, just like the hair in those commercials for a famous shampoo brand. Now that we've learned how to wield our staff in combat, we can expertly launch it forward, just like a javelin, reaching incredible distances. It carries a swift and intense energy, fueled by the power of our previous positive actions, which are now yielding results and propelling us along our path. It's like when you're playing a racing video game and you run over those arrows that give you a sudden burst of speed. While moving forward at such a rapid pace, we may not always be flawless, but it's the intention that matters. If our drive is fueled by the desire to progress, and if the moves we made before were aimed at self-improvement, then this is the sign or push we've been eagerly awaiting. Just be mindful of the target you're aiming for as you speed ahead! This card is generally quite positive but do watch out for an excessive presence of Swords, as they can destabilize this flight and send you plummeting into emptiness.

EIGHT OF CUPS: Imagine the number 8 as the track you follow along your journey. The central point, where the two curves of the number meet, is crucial in determining which turn to take and which direction to go. You've already covered half of the distance, and now you can embark on the other half or pause at the center to reflect on your next move. In this card, it's vital to be aware of the progress you've made so far and to assess whether the knowledge you've gained still serves you well. These factors play a key role in separating the two paths as distinct segments. It's time to take stock, much like when preparing for a trip and deciding what to pack. Will you bring the same items you packed last time, or can you shed some weight, knowing that you might miss those things during your journey? It's akin to deciding not to pack your fancy shoes, thinking you won't need them, only to be invited to a luxurious restaurant in the city where you're a guest. You might feel a bit lost or inadequate, but you can also proudly rock your sneakers because you know that the empty space in your suitcase can be filled with memories from the trip. This Eight sets you on a path to evaluate your past investments and set them aside while continuing to gather valuable growth experiences. Beware of potential obstacles or excessive regrets that may arise. Don't follow in the footsteps of Orpheus; trust the path that lies before you!

EIGHT OF SWORDS: In a parallel life, I was part of a band, and one of the songs I wrote had this verse: "Black bullets hurtle in my head, wires made of spiderwebs are binding my brain." It depicts the onslaught of negative thoughts intertwining and feeding off each other, representing the fears that hinder our progress, stemming from the anxiety of breaking free from something that seems constricting. If we were to open a drawer, would we find the scissors? Most certainly. But the question is, do we have the willingness to employ them? That's a separate matter altogether! We've reached a pivotal juncture, akin to a roller coaster train cresting the summit before hurtling downward. The void ahead may instill trepidation, yet it's the most exhilarating part of the entire journey, and it would be a shame to experience it with closed eyes. Be present in the moment when you allow your mind to unravel from the web of fears. Also, take heed of the subsequent cards: Are you the one entangling yourself, or do these ties originate externally or from others? How much sway do the fears of those around you hold, and how much solace do you genuinely find in remaining cocooned? Being raised by an overly apprehensive mother, I vividly recall that it was at the age of eight (how coincidental!) when I first conquered a slide, realizing that her fears had unwittingly hindered me earlier. Reflect on the role your own and others' fears play, and free yourself from their grip.

EIGHT OF PENTACLES: Raise your hand if you've ever listed "consistency" in the skills section of your résumé. Now, if you've recognized yourself in this description, then this card is all about you. You possess the remarkable ability to persevere in daily learning, constantly adding new knowledge to your repertoire and applying it with finesse in managing your expertise. Bravo! I must say, I do admire you a bit. The force and effort you put into your actions aren't over the top. It's not about going all out one day and then collapsing on the couch the next. No, instead, you have a steady approach to your daily endeavors. And if you see room for improvement, you apply yourself without rushing to compensate for what you've accomplished in the past. Think of it like friendships: there are those acquaintances who pop up once a year, then drown you in phone calls every day and all hours (or even less frequently, for that matter). And then there are those cherished friends who make their presence felt every single day through small but meaningful gestures. That's the kind of example that resonates with the Eight of

Pentacles. Picture yourself drawing a figure-eight with effortless fluidity: your pen glides quicker during the first curve, then seemingly pauses in the middle, but that's just a momentary illusion. In reality, your hand guides the pen to repeat another graceful curve, and the pattern continues infinitely. The more you repeat this shape, the better you become at drawing it smoothly. So, my friend, resist the temptation to rush. Otherwise, you might end up like that famous meme of the horse with exquisitely detailed hindquarters, as if it were sketched by Leonardo da Vinci himself, while the front end looks rather hastily drawn.

A PLAYLIST FOR EIGHTS
Walking Away—Craig David
Harder, Better, Faster, Stronger—Daft Punk
Spiderwebs—No Doubt
Move on Up—Curtis Mayfield

Still in doubt?
Consider how the four suits can be applied to Justice.

NINE OF SWORDS

NINE · On my own but in the world

NINE OF WANDS: In today's fast-paced world that demands high performance even from elementary school, with grandparents and parents telling us, "At your age, I was already married, owned a house, and had kids to take care of," always remember that many famous figures achieved success later in life. Age has nothing to do with success. For instance, in my birth chart, it suggests that I may reach my own success in adulthood (so, hey, support my dream by buying my book!). Take a moment to reflect on the journey you've undertaken so far, treasure the wealth of experience you've gained, including the inner transformation that allowed you to evolve and create all this with your own hands. As you recap the previous episodes, take a deep breath and observe the environment you've arrived in: it may differ greatly from your starting point, and it might even make you feel a bit disoriented initially, but that's normal. It all needs time to become familiar, so give yourself that adjustment period. You're standing on solid ground, so be patient and embrace the opportunity to soar when it presents itself. Now, what happens when you need to slow down? Do you sense external pressure urging you to rush through things, but only superficially? Ponder this thought, and if you notice that the cards around you suggest a lack of substance, then detach yourself from those influences.

NINE OF CUPS: Reaching a certain level of emotional awareness and taking care of it is an accomplishment that deserves to be celebrated. To do so, you've probably learned that you, Bae, must prioritize yourself and understand that constantly relying on others may not always be the best approach for personal or collective well-being. But now, you can truly be proud of what you have pursued. In the Three, the celebration was a shared experience, but here, at Nine, it's you who takes charge and organizes it, sharing your stories with those you choose, and relishing in the satisfaction and genuine joy of those who truly appreciate your success. The effort you've invested in your inner growth is now rewarded with the self-confidence that permeates your personal realm and guides the questions you ask (or are asked). After cutting out the unnecessary stuff with Eight, to make our progress smoother, what do we celebrate with the Nine and how do we share the fruits of all that we've learned up to this point? We're dealing with a really positive card here, but the only danger, if there are some not-so-nice cards nearby, is getting too full of ourselves and boasting about something we think we've achieved or understood. You know that feeling when you decide to start therapy or sign up for Zumba, and after the first appointment or class, you think you've got it all figured out? Well, that's pretty much the risk with Nine, unless there are other cards supporting your genuine growth and maturity.

NINE OF SWORDS: There are several things that can wake us up in the middle of the night: an external noise, a bad dream, or having eaten something heavy. Let's exclude the first and the last in this case and focus on the second. When we sleep, we come into contact with the innermost, inexplicable part of ourselves—the subconscious. Through dreams and seemingly incomprehensible visions, it tries to communicate with our consciousness to let us know that something is amiss or that there are unresolved knots from the past that we thought we had left behind. Thoughts are a powerful weapon; they can keep us awake at night or be like light bulbs that illuminate when we most need to find a solution to a thorny situation. Sometimes, we wish we could switch them off, especially when they take us back to moments we no longer wish to relive, while our brains seem to enjoy present-ing us with flashbacks, watching us from within with a bag of popcorn in hand as we agonize. The wisdom this card imparts is that despite our mind occasionally appearing as our fiercest adversary, the resources to conquer it and overcome the anguish inflicted by our own thoughts already reside within us. We mustn't shy away from introspection; instead, we should delve deep, testing our resilience, for without emotions and the ability to weather the night of ruminations, we risk being consumed by our own selves, much like certain cells resorting to self-cannibaliza-tion. Let us not be devoured by our own inner turmoil!

NINE OF PENTACLES: Ah, the satisfaction of having worked on yourself and your stability, to the point where you deserve that special treat, like being named the Employee of the Month (by yourself, of course). You've built up your inner wealth, brick by brick, tunnel after tunnel. You've known austerity in the past, endured moments of deprivation, delved deep within yourself under scorching sunlight and in the darkest, coldest nights. But now, Bae, it's time to truly relax. I mean, seriously. And hey, if you take a look around, you might just realize that you've left someone behind. Now is the moment to recognize that you've done an excellent job, appreciating and managing solitude. But it's also time to reintegrate into the world of sharing in every aspect of life—from communication to time, from wealth to emotions. Because let's face it, having an excess of solitary joys can start to feel a little sad and self-indulgent. It's only natural that you wanted to improve for your personal satisfaction, and it's absolutely valid. But at a certain point, embracing the art of sharing and reconnecting with the social fabric becomes essential. It's a way to avoid losing touch with the pleasure of collective experiences and to receive feedback that validates your positive personal journey.

A PLAYLIST FOR NINES

Quit Playing Games (With My Heart)—Backstreet Boys

Heavy—Linkin Park

One Step at a Time—Jordin Sparks

Try It on My Own—Whitney Houston

Still in doubt?
Consider how the four suits can be applied to the Hermit.

TEN OF PENTACLES

TEN · You've passed this level! (Sorry, but your princess is in another castle)

TEN OF WANDS: Luckily, we've reached the end of the numerical cycle because the fuel gauge is telling us we're running on empty and there's a risk of being stranded any moment now. Here, all the seeds you planted before have sprouted, and, speaking of Wands, they've grown into full-fledged bushes. Your desires have come to fruition. Well done, Bae, but now it's time to pause and let yourself be carried by the current. What comes after the appearance of this Arcanum in a reading? Cards of fulfillment or discontent? Do you still feel the need to toil excessively to feel complete, or are you forgetting to appreciate the achieved results? The fiery energy can make you hyperactive, but sometimes true fulfillment lies in recognizing when it's time to stop before starting anew. Otherwise, there won't be a clear distinction between the end and the beginning of a project, a journey, or a new phase within a relationship. They say "too much of a good thing can be detrimental," so keep that in mind when this card crosses your path and try to heed the advice it brings: reflect on your journey, take satisfaction in what you've accomplished, and embark on a new adventure. Just like Super Mario, who strives to progress from one level to the next only to find out that Princess Peach is still in another place, you'll need to make further efforts to rescue her. But for now, be content with planting your flag.

TEN OF CUPS: We've truly grasped the significance of community and embracing a personal realm that encompasses our relationships in the Nine. From the very beginning, starting with the Ace, we've multiplied our Cups, filling them to the brim with fluid emotions, at times overflowing without reserve, and other times letting them dry up or spill away. Now we find ourselves in a state of perfect balance, where the glass is neither half full nor half empty—it simply exists. Personal fulfillment has the power to radiate outward like shimmering stardust, affecting everyone within our circle. This card brings forth triumph and achievements in all areas, but how far are you willing to challenge yourself to attain this state of semi-beatification? The presence of Swords cards alongside the Ten of Cups, signifying conflicts or struggles, reminds us that nothing is everlasting and that reaching our desires exacts a price. Are we prepared to pay that price through both favorable and trying times?

TEN OF SWORDS: This is the card that represents when, after enduring a seemingly endless marathon in a truly hostile environment, we witness the exhausted athlete crawling on their elbows toward the finish line, just like in that marathon scene from the movie *Super Fantozzi*. Finally, it's over! You can let out a sigh of relief, and trust me, it won't be the last one. While it may not be the most thrilling Arcanum, it does bring something valuable: after every ending, even if there isn't much to celebrate, there's a fresh start waiting for you. That's where you should focus your energy. If you've made a mess, hit rock bottom, or feel like your race has come to an bad end, the final battle and surrender also highlight the importance of embracing a new concept: resignation. This doesn't mean wallowing in self-pity but rather picking yourself up. As the band Afterhours sang, "Your diploma in failure is a degree in resilience." So, in which area of your life have you earned this certificate? Take a moment to reflect on how you carry your wounds and your relationship with mistakes. Can you forge ahead on your own two feet, or do you find yourself crawling, almost seeking punishment? Are you able to see errors as part of the learning process?

TEN OF PENTACLES: Always think of the number Ten as fulfillment: what I've described in pages and pages as the "achievement of your goal" finally comes to pass. You have all the puzzle pieces in your hands, and your stability is reached. Now you can truly say it out loud and message all your loved ones who are coming to gather around you and sing your praises throughout the kingdom. The appearance of this Arcanum indicates that you can become very popular in what you do, and this can bring you an abundance of esteem, as well as gains that can be translated into both economic and human terms. You can forge new bonds through the dissemination of your skills and the desire to create a community based on mutual commitment and respect in the area of life where the question is posed and where this card makes its appearance. When it comes to feelings, the way we love our partner, our friends, or our family is full, mature, and protective. In the professional field, we are truly on point. We have the support of colleagues and clients, and we are ready to dive headfirst into new projects. In both sectors, we find ourselves in well-established situations where we move with perfect ease. However, if in a spread there are an excessive number of Pentacle cards alongside this Ten, be wary of gilded cages. We may become so comfortable in our current state that we resist embarking on a new cycle, risking becoming rigid and possessive, unable to embrace change and growth.

Still in doubt?
Consider how the four suits can be applied to the Wheel of Fortune.

PAGE OF SWORDS

PAGE · Forever young

PAGE OF WANDS: A friend who always knows how to make you laugh, who convinces you to embark on spontaneous train journeys across the country, who follows a path forged by someone else and decides to make it their own. When the Page of Wands appears in a Tarot reading, it signifies a promising display of initiative. We are discovering how to use our own talents and passions to illuminate our potential, inspiring others to do the same.

I envision this Arcanum as a modern-day TikToker, whose communication style is attuned to the times, and whose innovative ideas quickly become viral, serving as a wellspring of inspiration for their peers. Take, for instance, Sinister, the creator who transformed their love for fragrances into a genuine mission, breathing new life into an otherwise mundane industry, making it captivating and appealing to the younger generation.

So, what can we expect when encountering this Arcanum? Undoubtedly, a surge of energy in various aspects of life, a keen desire to approach goals with a fresh and enthusiastic mindset. We infuse our endeavors with a strong sense of personal initiative, leaving a lasting imprint and ensuring that we are remembered. However, it's essential to keep the flame burning bright. The pitfall of the "youthful spirit" cards lies in inconsistency, the waning of initial excitement for a specific endeavor, and a lack of patience that hampers complete growth.

My advice? Find inspiration in the unwavering commitment of someone who can serve as a role model, a figure to aspire to, while maintaining your own individuality and avoiding excessive influence. Keep your focus sharp by incorporating stimulating ideas into your projects, preventing distractions from diverting your attention away from your distant goals.

PAGE OF CUPS: Our mind is capable of giving life to incredibly imaginative images, adding additional levels of perceptual experience to the tangible reality that allow us to broaden our perspective on exciting worlds. Think of the works of painters and filmmakers, or consider the work of fashion designers who, starting from the necessity of clothing the body, create true dreams, opening up a parallel dimension of creativity and expressiveness for a daily object like clothes. The Page of Cups urges you to bring forth your visions, to transform them into reality—the most delightful reality you can manifest—and to fall deeply in love with it, allowing yourself to fully connect and merge with your creation. But don't keep it all to yourself; offer it up, share it with others, and invite them to partake from the cup overflowing with the passion and dedication you pour into your endeavors. The heart and mind of this Page resemble an amusement park, where you infuse your ideals and recreate the same exhilaration you feel when witnessing a fantastical parade or riding a roller coaster for the first time.

The Page of Cups brings to mind the great Michael Jackson, whose immense and visionary artistic talent was accompanied by a spirit that remained eternally youthful. The wisdom this card imparts is to avoid being swept away by dreams without restraint. Allow your emotions the time and space to mature, and take care of the things and people you fall in love with, whether it's a project, a transformative change, or a relationship.

PAGE OF SWORDS: This Page embodies the moral qualities, ambitions, and abilities reminiscent of Harry Potter, who, throughout the various chapters of his story, learns to defend himself, seek the truth about his past, and wield magic for noble purposes. This Page's mind is receptive to new ways of thinking, and their actions are driven by the insatiable desire to acquire knowledge. It's like when you meet someone at a gathering and instinctively turn to social media to uncover their life and perhaps reach out to them. Yes, that's what the Page of Swords would do. Or it's that feeling you get when someone tells you a blatant falsehood, and you become like Miss Marple, determined to bring the truth to light (even if it was just a harmless fib, you despise deceit). If you're a fan of puzzle games, this card represents the kind of intelligence you employ to solve them—a particular kind of dedication, keen attention to detail, and the mental agility required to unravel their mysteries.

Often, behind this Page, there lies a challenge or obstacle that needs to be overcome or cut through, and it is from this necessity that this Arcanum emerges. So, heighten your senses, seek out the elements that can aid you as you pursue your investigation or mission, and trust in your sharpness of mind. However, be cautious not to succumb to arrogance! This card brings to mind the tendency of younger generations to question or challenge the words or impositions of their predecessors. They are the children who rebelliously yet positively defy their parents, the spirit of improvisation that enters academia, upending its conventional wisdom in favor of a more contemporary style of education, both in form and content. The important thing is to always strive for the highest form of reasoning and not to be enticed by the power that the mind sometimes wields, using it for less than noble purposes, such as spinning elaborate lies or playing games with unfair tactics.

PAGE OF PENTACLES: This card represents those who dive headfirst into a venture, fueled by the burning desire to make a splash in their chosen field, wherever this Arcanum has made its presence felt. The Page, with their gigantic coin, serves as a reminder that if you truly want to see results, you must power down your phone, eliminate all distractions, and delve deep in the direction of your aspirations. But make no mistake, this figure isn't about self-denial—don't envision them as a Buddhist monk. Their goal is to secure a bright future, and they do so through unwavering dedication, not self-flagellation. They revel in what they've chosen to pursue, fueled by the excitement of discovering their talents day by day, honing them to perfection.

You know that feeling when you embark on a new course (like a Tarot class, for instance) and find yourself completely immersed in a tunnel of enthusiasm and concentration, only emerging once you feel you've become a true expert in that subject? Or when you meet someone new and an insatiable curiosity takes hold, driving you to spend as much time as possible together, sensing that this connection could become a pivotal force in your personal growth? That's the very essence of this Arcanum.

However, if there are cards in the spread that bring forth blocks or insecurities, then we find ourselves unable to fully grasp our own potential. We may lack a specific passion or struggle to take that leap forward, the one that propels an interest to become something truly meaningful on our unique journey.

A PLAYLIST FOR THE PAGES
ABC—The Jackson 5
Rome Wasn't Built in a Day—Morcheeba

SONGS FROM ITALY
Giovani Wannabe—Pinguini Tattici Nucleari
Giudizi Universali—Samuele Bersani

KNIGHT OF PENTACLES

There is a message
for you · KNIGHT

KNIGHT OF WANDS: Have you ever seen the movie *Thelma and Louise*? It always comes to mind when I see this card! It's about two friends who, tired with their mundane lives and suffocated by their partners, embark on a wild spontaneous adventure. They end up getting into all sorts of crazy situations driven by their impulses and the desire to reclaim their lives. They run from the police and encounter some rather questionable characters along the way.

But it also reminds me of the Quidditch Seekers, made famous by the Harry Potter saga. These players must chase and capture the elusive Golden Snitch, zooming at breakneck speed, skillfully handling their brooms with daring maneuvers, trying to avoid crashing to the ground but often coming dangerously close to it.

Do you get the energy of this card now? By combining the fiery element of the Wands with the airy nature of the Knights, we're dealing with an incredible surge of physical energy. It's all about following our instincts and taking action fueled by our desires. With such vigor, staying still is nearly impossible! If there's something you truly long for, go ahead and seize it! The object of desire depends on the question at hand.

Keep an eye on what card comes after this Knight, as it'll show us if all this enthusiasm is wisely directed or if we're getting carried away by questionable endeavors that might not be right for us at the moment. This card's energy can also help us understand if we need a change of direction in any aspect of our lives.

For instance, let's say, in our family life, we've been stuck in old patterns of behavior. The Knight of Wands encourages us to find the strength to break free and be different from our parents. And if we've always relied on others at work to tell us what to do, it's time to be more independent!

KNIGHT OF CUPS: Knights are all about delivering messages, and Cups represent the realm of feelings and emotions. Now, when you bring these two together, you get an Arcana that nudges us to break free from our mental and physical boundaries and express our innermost emotions to the world around us. It's like those middle school days when we'd pass notes to our classmates, asking, "Do you want to be with me? YES / NO." Talk about emotional bravery! (I was twenty-five when I finally got over those "no" responses.)

But the Knight of Cups is fearless when it comes to wearing their heart on their sleeve. Whether those messages are directed at us or dear Ms. Betty, whether they come from the outside world, be it a compliment, a supportive gesture, or a heart-felt declaration of love, they're all ready to be expressed openly.

And let me tell you, the words we choose to convey those feelings will be sweet and tender, just like those little love notes that are inside the wrappers of the Italian *Baci Perugina* chocolates or a thoughtful colleague leaving Post-it notes for us on our computer. It's all about genuine "I'm sorry" and "I love you" moments that truly touch the heart.

So, here's the thing: how do we feel about expressing affection? Are we hesitant, are we comfortable with it, or do we use it as a way to get something in return? This card prompts us to ponder this aspect and consider its significance for ourselves and the people involved in the question we're exploring.

KNIGHT OF SWORDS: It's time for everything you've been holding back until now to find its way out. I mean, let's be honest, it's up to you to make it happen. As you've probably realized (and as you'll explain to Ms. Betty too), things don't just magically fall into place. Those situations that bothered you, the little white lies you told to get out of trouble or end a heated discussion, and the injustice you've witnessed or faced—it's time to come out with it! Remember what Shrek said, "Better out than in," especially when it comes to words or thoughts that slowly poison our minds. Personally, I've always believed in speaking the truth because every time I've lied or withheld something important, it's led to unpleasant conse-quences. I don't want those heavy situations to repeat themselves because of my silence or dishonesty. So go ahead and let it out, be honest, and free yourself from all that burden. This Arcana teaches us the art of voicing our concerns in a just cause, urging us not to shy away from using our intelligence and critical thinking to shed light on situations that appear unclear or unjust. It prompts us to follow our moral compass when we witness something, or someone threatened by forces com-promising their authenticity. For example, if someone tries to tarnish the reputation of someone dear to us or seeks to take advantage, we waste no time in unmasking the truth and speaking out boldly.

However, I must offer a word of caution: while speaking the truth is vital, we must not use it as an excuse to be harsh or sow discord. Unfortunately, this could happen all too easily with this Arcana's influence. Our true aim lies in seeking justice and displaying nobility of character by presenting reality as it is. Are we sincere in upholding these values, or do we merely boast about our intelligence without possessing even a shred of emotional intelligence?

KNIGHT OF PENTACLES: This Arcana stirs up conflicting feelings in me, perhaps because when I was young, I used to be as slow as molasses, but now, sometimes, I'm like a lightning bolt and can't stand wishy-washy people. This Knight isn't exactly wishy-washy either; they're more cautious, wanting to do things right, bringing the right materials to build your project or relationship, step by step. It takes time to find it, transport it, assemble the right team, and find the perfect ground to build upon. But in the end, the finished work stands tall like the Burj Khalifa, strong like the Colosseum, and as delightful as a *finca* in the hinterland of Ibiza.

This card exudes a constant and dependable energy, so it's never a good idea to act on a whim or take on a commitment without being sure. There's no need to rush but pay attention to the useful details as you move forward in the area indicated by the question. Save some reserves and don't give everything away to people you've just met. Consider what this attitude might bring in return as you analyze this card.

A PLAYLIST FOR THE KNIGHTS
I Love You—Woodkid
Unstoppable—Sia
Moving in the Right Direction—Gossip

SONGS FROM ITALY
Ci Vuole un Fiore—Sergio Endrigo

QUEEN OF WANDS

The QUEEN of my castle

QUEEN OF WANDS: This Queen is an absolute icon: dressed to kill, exuding a confident aura, and fully aware of her irresistible charm. She commands respect from her loyal subjects without instilling terror. She's emerged victorious from countless battles, and if I were to use a cliché, I'd say she was "thrown into the wolves' den and emerged as their alpha." This figure has the power to inspire the masses, instilling a sense of security and courage in those fortunate enough to cross her path. She embraces her sexuality unabashedly, without succumbing to moralistic judgments or engaging in relationships solely for the sake of justifying her vibrant sensuality.

Tap into the energy of this card when you need to seize control of your life and make decisions for yourself, disregarding the expectations others place upon you. You are in the driver's seat; be your own guide and encourage those around you to follow suit! You possess the adaptability to extract the best from every experience, whether it be relationships, work dynamics, or personal growth. This Arcanum reminds me of Wonder Woman, the fierce superheroine of the Justice League. She wields incredible power but also possesses innate leadership skills. She is not driven by violence or a thirst for revenge; instead, she discerns when to fight for her ideals or to maintain peace. Despite her impulsive nature, she knows when to pause and reflect for the greater good.

However, when the Queen of Wands appears alongside other Wands or Swords cards, her darker side emerges, characterized by excessive assertiveness, bullying tendencies, and arrogance. This can make her particularly aggressive in certain situations and when engaging with others. The advice from this card is to find true passion, embrace a cause, and fight for the love of your individuality or a meaningful relationship while staying true to your moral compass.

QUEEN OF CUPS: I had been hoping for the perfect moment to write or speak these words aloud: whenever I gaze upon the portrayal of the Queen of Cups in the Rider-Waite-Smith deck, I cannot help but see Lady Diana Spencer. To me, this Arcanum not only bears a striking resemblance to her in appearance, but it also captures the essence of her public persona during her time among us. Whenever this card emerges, our ability to fall head over heels for something or someone knows no bounds. Our sensitivity toward the world that surrounds us becomes finely tuned, as does our inclination to surround ourselves with all things beautiful and delightful, both for the eyes and the spirit.

We have come to a point where we are fully capable of nurturing the aspect of life indicated by the question posed, to the point where we feel as though it is our very own creation, one to be protected and defended at any cost. Our emotional landscape tends to be harmonious, as does our relationship with spirituality and inner well-being. Just imagine immersing yourself in a warm bath, relishing the cocooning sensation as the water envelops and embraces you—that is precisely what encountering (or embodying) the Queen of Cups feels like.

To love and actively perceive the object of our desires, transcending mere physical necessity and focusing primarily on a more elevated plane—this is the very heart of this Arcanum. Yet, it also encompasses something more profound. It entails experiencing the battles and sorrows of others as if they were our own. We become the greatest champions of our family, friends, or partners. However, we must also consider our own needs and not solely live to please others. The sensitivity with which we are endowed intensifies every sensation, making the suffering of others become our own, and any harm inflicted upon us by others has profound repercussions on our emotional well-being. The shadow of the Queen of Cups resides in her boundless capacity for endurance, which can transform into self-inflicted suffering. This card consumes us from within, as all the tools we could use to save ourselves are within our grasp, awaiting the spark of self-preservation to set them in motion. The advice carried by this Arcanum is to cherish the value of our sensitivity, our talents, and our ability to nurture, all while keeping in mind that to truly thrive, we must first tend to the well-being of our own hearts.

QUEEN OF SWORDS: With an exceptionally high intelligence quotient, profound analytical abilities, and keen observation skills, she could be an international spy, a lawyer, or a passionate human rights activist. The Queen of this suit goes straight to the heart of the matter, possessing an enviable eloquence that she employs to dissect situations with precision and excel in debates.

Trust me, you wouldn't want to engage in an argument with her, for she has a knack for presenting all the reasons against you, leaving no doubt about her rightness. She is your staunch ally when it comes to examining a situation from a rational perspective, providing you with effective responses, or delivering unadulterated truths. Naturally, she may not appeal to everyone, but she couldn't care less about public approval; her aim is to convey things as they truly are. However, this Queen's Achilles' heel is her propensity to transition from being forthright to being somewhat caustic. She may derive great pleasure from indulging in gossip or uttering a cutting remark simply for the sake of it (even though there is a tactful way to express oneself, even when rooted in truth). In a negative light, particularly when surrounded by numerous Swords cards, she brings to mind Regina George from *Mean Girls*—an embodiment of snobbishness and a sharp tongue. Given her association with the Air element, there is a risk of failing to let thoughts settle and impulsively making snide remarks without considering the consequences. The wisdom of this Arcanum advises against using one's intelligence to belittle others but rather to strive for unwavering justice that is fiercely defended.

QUEEN OF PENTACLES: She governs over the element of Earth. Practical and grounded, she stands tall as a sturdy pillar, capable of achieving great things even with limited resources. While she may appear somewhat austere, I assure you that her greatest fulfillment comes from rolling up her sleeves, first securing stability, and then learning to appreciate more than what she initially set out to possess. Her boundaries are meticulously maintained and well-defined, and within them, one finds every form of comfort, leaving no deficiency for herself or those fortunate enough to receive an invitation to cross her threshold.

This Queen is an entrepreneur, blessed with a keen business acumen. She cannot be swayed by empty promises but instead focuses on tangible results that her unwavering dedication brings forth in every endeavor she undertakes. Miuccia Prada, with her clean and essential style, transformed a family business into an iconic pillar of the international fashion world. Csaba dalla Zorza, a renowned Italian food writer and chef with her impeccable taste in hospitality, elevated her career as a chef, turning the ritual of food into a true art form. These two individuals embody the essence of the Queen of Pentacles, driven by a profound passion for something deeply rooted in the material realm, such as fashion or cuisine. They reach the pinnacle of success through specific actions and targeted strategies aimed at excellence and the establishment of a genuine empire.

This Arcanum holds a positive influence when accompanied by other positive Arcana. However, without such accompaniment, it can easily devolve into a mere display of material gains as empty status symbols. When surrounded by dominant cards, it becomes a contest of who can outshine the rest, dissipating energy in superficial and hollow ways, simply to "possess" others or assert dominance with pride and a hint of arrogance.

The advice brought forth by this card is to learn the art of resource management, leading us toward a state of financial security. Once we achieve such stability, we can then share our wealth, recognizing that generosity should not serve as a means to feel magnanimous, but rather as a way to share the surplus we perceive.

A PLAYLIST FOR THE QUEENS
Born to Make You Happy—Britney Spears
Fossora—Björk
I Was an Eagle—Laura Marling

SONGS FROM ITALY
Aggiungi un Posto a Tavola—Johnny Dorelli

KING OF CUPS

I will make you into a KING

KING OF WANDS: The King's overwhelming nature and unwavering authenticity are the very qualities that have propelled him to success. He is a figure who evokes either love or hatred, leaving no room for lukewarm feelings. This Arcanum strongly brings to mind the persona of Evita Perón, one of Argentina's most influential figures in politics and society. She had the remarkable ability to inspire and amplify the voices of the nation's poorest and its women, commanding credibility, strength, and charisma. This card beckons you to take a firm stance, to remain true to your ideals, and to fear nothing. In fact, if there is something or someone you fear, let that fear serve as the fuel to unlock your full potential and determination in any battle you face. Passion is the driving force behind this King; he is unpretentious and straightforward. Within his exuberance and boisterous demeanor lies a profound awareness that these very qualities have set him apart amidst a sea of uniformity. This card urges you to embrace a style that authentically represents you, rather than conforming to societal norms. It encourages you to deliver an exam with a captivating and contrarian speech, diverging from the flawless yet mundane response of another student. It implores you to effect genuine change within a relationship, avoiding hollow promises that perpetuate without fulfillment. How can you rise above and alter the course of a seemingly doomed dynamic? Reflect on how you can unleash your full potential and summon the courage needed to confront any challenge head-on.

KING OF CUPS: This King can read you like an open book, understanding every aspect of your being. Who you are, what you feel, and what drives you—he can't be fooled. If he senses you're about to make a move, he'll know it before you can even imagine it. His intuition is his greatest ally, flawlessly guiding him alongside his emotions, of which he is an expert interpreter. He fully embraces and experiences them. When this card appears in a reading, it urges you to learn from his example, to fearlessly embrace the depths of your emotions, whether they bring heavenly bliss or troubling concerns. The world of internal sensations should be savored in its entirety, even if it takes on a mystical quality. In fact, that's precisely why you should dive in headfirst! Granted, this may lead to emotional roller coasters, but only through this process can you learn to navigate the tides of your own moods. Have you ever attended a concert of your absolute favorite artist? How did you feel when you saw them take the stage? What emotions did you experience upon receiving news of a job loss or the passing of a loved one? How did you react in those situations? This card urges you not to suppress your feelings, but to embrace them as a driving force, proudly displaying them, even if some may perceive them as weaknesses and mock you within the context you find yourself in. It's like watching a powerful, emotional movie with your closest friends, feeling the tears welling up and the urge to let them flow. Don't be ashamed; let yourself have a cathartic cry. There's nothing wrong with expressing your vulnerabilities without questioning your worth. On the other hand, if this card appears alongside others indicating a challenging relationship with emotions, there's a risk of being unable to engage in a discussion without tears or losing control over your sensations, allowing them to overwhelm you, when instead, you should be the one guiding them.

KING OF SWORDS: If you're the kind of person who meticulously analyzes every situation and gesture, approaching them with mathematical precision, and if you combine empirical data with the confirmations that daily observations and intuition provide, then you'll find this card appealing. It embodies a remarkably high level of intellectual maturity and leaves little room for error in its assessments. It's the quintessential card that perfectly captures those who often say, "I told you so," when faced with a situation that ended poorly but could have easily been avoided had people just used their heads. The crucial point to remember is that when these reproachful words are uttered, they stem from genuine concern for the person involved, rather than a desire to assert superiority or relish in the missteps of others. This card urges us to embrace logic, to unleash the full potential of our mental faculties, and to strategically ponder solutions that align closely with the concept of justice. This is especially important when someone involved in the situation being scrutinized by the question is driven by self-interest, perhaps even resorting to deceitful means. The King of Swords is not easily swayed or bought. He remains impervious to seductive allure and cannot be convinced to follow the wrong path simply because others are going that way. He remains steadfast and loyal, and it is precisely these qualities that enable him to find the right ally in his battle. Ask yourself: "Would I rather be a lone voice standing up for what's right, even if it means being in the minority, or would I prefer to blend in with the crowd like a sheep, simply to avoid feeling out of place, even if I don't share their principles or ideas?" Remember, swords are meant to cut, and in this card, it signifies the need to separate morally upright ideas from the mediocre opinions of the majority. It's about carefully examining the facts that help us determine whether a relationship is worth maintaining, evaluating the actions we take to achieve our goals, and measuring their actual effectiveness. This King must constantly strive for an ethical ideal to avoid misusing his power and intelligence, ensuring he doesn't become a dictator who relies solely on cunning strategies and low blows.

KING OF PENTACLES: Oh, this King is doing so well, my friend, you can't even imagine! In the theory of manifesting, we possess the power of individual will that allows us to bring our wildest dreams to life. It's a combination of visualizing our desires in advance and taking concrete actions to make them a reality. And let me tell you, the King of Pentacles must have mastered the art of manifesting from his early days as a mere Magician. His success didn't come from merely envisioning the future, but from wholeheartedly dedicating himself to each present moment. This unwavering focus grounded him firmly and propelled him forward.

As you know, the energy of Pentacles may not be swift, but it possesses an extraordinary quality: it is solid and unwavering. When this card appears, it urges you to embody these very qualities. Whether you're seeking to support a loved one or striving for a new job opportunity, what matters most is your intention to pursue it and the consistent steps you take to make it happen. Even in seemingly trivial matters like changing your appearance or organizing your wardrobe for a new season, this card advises you to do it with utmost care, one step at a time, making intelligent investments of your time and resources.

Now, let me ask you this: When you truly desire something or aim to be a pillar of support for someone, do you approach it with steady determination? Or do you constantly seek external validation and stimulation, easily becoming distracted by the first shiny diversion that comes your way? Another aspect to consider is the potential danger of becoming fixated on stability. When you set your sights on a goal or ambition, do you stubbornly cling to your original plan, or are you flexible enough to adapt when circumstances change?

A PLAYLIST FOR THE KINGS
Golden Touch—Razorlight
I Want It All—Queen
Underwater Love—Smoke City

SONGS FROM ITALY
Le Tue Parole Fanno Male—Cesare Cremonini

When to use the Major Arcana and when to use the Minor Arcana

Once you have mastered the Major Arcana and their meanings, you may already have everything you need to read Tarot cards and offer in-depth interpretations. With the Major Arcana, you can explore various concepts and delve into each card for ten minutes or more. However, what if you need a precise and sharp response, or if you want to add some details in case the reading with the Major Arcana provided a too general overview and you still have doubts about the topic? That's when we bring out our 56 Minor Arcana cards!

Each card in the Minor Arcana expresses limited meanings, but we shouldn't think of this adjective negatively. On the contrary, it can be quite beneficial. While the Major Arcana provide a broader perspective and sometimes even risk going off track, the Minor Arcana cards make it easier to stay focused and go into detail about the situation. Personally, I'm not a fan of mixing the Major and Minor Arcana in a spread. It's because the Minor Arcana sometimes cover similar meanings and aspects found in the Majors, but in a more condensed way. It feels like repeating the same concept but with fewer words. So, I prefer to separate them based on the question at hand. If I need to address general inquiries or create spreads that span a significant period of time, such as questions about personal growth or when various factors influence a specific situation, I rely on the Major Arcana. They offer a more comprehensive view, considering multiple aspects. However, when it comes to lighter or less psychologically impactful queries, the Minor Arcana can be quite useful. They allow me to track the progression of a situation without constantly invoking the grandeur of the Majors. It's all about tailoring the approach and providing Ms. Betty with a thorough answer that takes into account all relevant factors. I use the Minor Arcana in the weekly spreads that I post on my Instagram account, the famous "Spreadie of the Redie." They allow me to convey brief concepts in a short amount of time and provide answers to questions about lighthearted topics in everyday life. They also serve as additional advice to a spread where I've used the Major Arcana. Unlike the Majors, I exclusively read the Minors upright because I use them as prompts for reflection or as guidance on navigating daily dynamics.

The Major Arcana form the structure, the unfolding story that delves into the depths with each card. They provide profound insights. On the other hand, the Minor Arcana act as punctuation, adding details and nuances. Depending on the suit, they can suggest whether we're in the realm of emotions, practicality, intellect, or material matters. Let me give you another straightforward example to help you understand the difference: the Majors are like us, representing our personality, backbone, and personal growth. The Minors are like the accessories we wear—our clothes, makeup, and stylistic choices that enhance who we already are. They can change our appearance and alter our life's path, but deep down, we remain true to ourselves.

Let's get our hands dirty

Dear Bae, you've probably either read this tome—a product of my experience and my pop delusions—in one breath, devouring it completely or maybe you've savored it like a cocktail at an aperitif bar as you watched the sun gracefully set over the breathtaking Ionian coast, totally relaxed and in complete bliss. However you chose to indulge, I'm here to tell you that now is the time to put your plans into action, awaken your mind, unlock the power of your seventh chakra, and apply what you've learned. Welcome to the exercise section.

Within these pages, you'll discover four types of exercises: closed questions, open questions, creating your own personalized spreads, and utilizing keywords. And that's not all! At the end, there are two dynamic exercises and a delightful surprise awaiting you. Now, I've deliberately chosen not to provide personal interpretations or examples of resolution. Why, you may ask? Because cartomancy is not a rigid doctrine, and my intention is to empower your intuition and allow the meanings stored within your memory to unfold naturally.

So, my dear, grab your favorite deck and let the journey begin!

CLOSED QUESTIONS: I will present you with a situation: a hypothetical question posed by Ms. Betty, along with the cards that have been drawn in the spread. Your task is to provide an interpretation, starting with the surface meanings and gradually delving deeper. Pay close attention to how the various Arcana interact with each other, and whether the numbers indicate progression or regression.

· Ms. Betty wants to know how she can move on after a failed relationship. The cards drawn are Judgment upright, the Moon upright, the Magician reversed, and the Sun upright. The cards are arranged in the cross spread, which you can find in the "Spreads and Methods of Tarot Reading" section.

· Ms. Betty has a stable and routine job that somewhat satisfies her, and she also has a parallel photography project that occasionally brings in some income and is slowly expanding. She wants to know whether she should continue with her current profession or become a wedding photographer. The cards are arranged in the V spread, which you can find in the "Spreads and Methods of Tarot Reading" section, and they are as follows: on the left, representing her current profession, we have the Four of Wands, the Nine of Pentacles, and the Page of Wands; on the right, representing the photography project, we have the Ace of Wands, the Five of Cups, and the Queen of Cups. How would you describe these two situations, and consequently, what advice would you give to Ms. Betty? Should she stay or should she go?

· Ms. Betty has been running a business for about a year, but she expected a much higher flow of customers. She asks what she is doing wrong and how she can improve her business. The cards that come up are the Magician upright, Temperance reversed, the Emperor reversed, and the Hierophant upright. What would you tell her in response, and what suggestions would you give her based on the cards that came up?

· Ms. Betty has to face a job interview for a position similar to her previous one. She would like some tips on how to present herself and which aspects she might be more at risk of failure in. The cards drawn are the Fool upright, Justice upright, the Moon reversed, and the Lovers reversed. What can she leverage and what should she pay attention to?

· Our beloved Ms. Betty is in a relationship that seems to have reached a point of no return. After seven years together, she feels that there are many differences, but clearly not enough effort has been made to bridge them. The cards that come up are the Chariot reversed, the Lovers reversed, the Magician upright, and the Sun upright. Is it worth giving it another try or is it better to cut ties? Why?

· Ms. Betty wants to get a makeover, cut her hair, do something that makes her feel different. She asks whether she should make some adjustments or stay as she is, and the cards that come up are the Eight of Cups, the Ace of Swords, the Seven of Cups, and the Queen of Pentacles. Would you recommend this change of look or is it better to avoid it?

OPEN QUESTIONS: Naturally, in addition to all the questions you want to ask your cards, try practicing with the ones I propose below! Again, interpret the cards you draw as answers to the questions without digressing—don't lose the thread of the conversation, and avoid giving overly imaginative interpretations.

· Ms. Betty (who else could it be?) is about to inherit a sum of money, but it also comes with a portion of debts that she would have to pay out of her own pocket. She asks whether it's worthwhile for her to accept the inheritance or refuse it, and why.

· Ms. Betty is going through a period of significant changes, first with her housing situation, and now with her job. She would like to know how to navigate this new path. Please draw some cards for her.

· Ms. Betty aspires to a peaceful romantic relationship but finds herself consistently pursuing the same type of individuals who are generally emotionally unavailable.

Through the Tarot, she seeks to understand why this keeps happening and how she can break free from this cycle.

· Torn between a path of legal studies and one in acting, a very confused Ms. Betty asks you to help her understand which path can prove to be the best in terms of ambitions and the challenges she may face.

· While waiting to decide whether to rent an apartment or buy one, Ms. Betty wants to know which of the two options might be better in the short term. Lay out the cards to provide her with the most suitable suggestion for her current situation.

· This period for Ms. Betty seems to be full of challenges: she is torn between a love that has come to an end and the desire to get to know someone who has recently entered her life, even though it may seem too soon to dive headfirst into a new relationship. Use the Tarot cards to provide her with guidance on how to handle this situation.

MAKE SOME SPREADS: As I mentioned in the dedicated chapter, coming up with custom spreads can be incredibly useful in providing an ideal structure tailored to the specific needs arising from the type of question you're asked. It can also prove valuable during certain times of the year, such as your birthday, lunar cycles, planetary transits, and more. I'll provide you with a list of themes, and you can create spreads that best suit your desired advice, incorporating the format and key points that resonate with you. If you'd like, feel free to share them on Instagram, tagging me and using the hashtag *#leSpreadDelleAme*!

· Ms. Betty wants to have a Tarot reading, but she doesn't know what to ask specifically. Create a spread dedicated to all the unprepared Ms. Betties or those having their first experience.

· The new year has just started, and you want to try to see what kind of projects await you or what new paths you can take. Create a spread with this type of energy, something that gives you the motivation to start a new cycle.

· What shape would you give a spread that can provide advice on how to manifest an idea or a dream?

· Create a spread layout that you would use to plan something in your life, anything at all.

· Use your imagination to create a freeform layout for any Tarot experiment that comes to mind!

KEYWORDS: Use your intuition, look at the images, immerse yourself in the card. I'll give you the context and the card that comes up. Write down as quickly as possible the first concepts or keywords that come to mind.

· You wake up in the morning and try to understand what the dominant energy of your day might be. You draw the Knight of Cups. Jot down at least four keywords to describe the course of the day that is beginning.

· Ms. Betty has indulged in reckless shopping and asks for advice on how to save some money. The Three of Wands is drawn. What comes to mind right away?

· Ms. Betty would like to open her relationship to other partners and seeks advice on how to approach and discuss it with her current partner. The Devil card is drawn. How can she address the conversation? Express the concept with the first words that come to mind.

· Ms. Betty is very fond of her cat and is considering getting another one. She is unsure if it's the right time, so she asks for an opinion. The reversed Empress card is drawn. What do you think of her idea? Share a few quick insights.

· On the street, you find a Ten of Swords card. What do you think it's trying to tell you? Think of the first keywords that come to mind with this card.

· To complete a certain spiritual journey, the advice card drawn in a reading is the Six of Swords. What actions can be taken to facilitate this evolution? Express it with the first meanings that emerge in your mind.

GROUPING EXERCISE: This is an activity you can do when observing the Tarot cards you have drawn in a spread. We can identify some major groups of cards, united by similar characteristics: Movement, Emotion, Sociality, Introspection, Change, and so on. Create your own macro-categories that, in your opinion, can encompass multiple cards, while trying to include all 78 cards. This exercise stimulates your mind to find a common thread within the reading. Observe the Arcana: How many speak of Sociality? Are there more cards related to the concept of Change, or do you find that the main theme uniting them is Stability? This practice is super helpful because it helps you find the focal point on which to concentrate your interpretation, and it also assists the querent in clearly understanding what they need to work on.

SIMILARITIES: This is an exercise that can help you train your memory. It's important to approach it with flexibility rather than strict rules. The goal is to create connections and associations between the Major and Minor Arcana, focusing on similarities rather than exact matches (hence the name "Similarities" instead of "Exact Matches"). Here's how you can do it: Start with the Major Arcana, as they hold deeper meanings. Identify any Minor Arcana cards that share common themes or symbolism with the Majors. For a hands-on approach, lay out all the Major

Arcana cards on a table and place the corresponding Minor Arcana cards on top of them, noting down your reasons for the connections in a notebook. Revisit the exercise after a few months and see if you still agree with your initial associations or if you would make any changes. This practice allows you to explore the relationships between the cards and deepen your understanding over time.

Postscript to the exercises, or a letter for you, Bae.

Remember that reading Tarot cards is like riding a bike: the more you do it, the better you get. And there are plenty of other activities that follow this rule. Doing Tarot readings is definitely one of them because with each session, your brain picks up countless additional nuances. So go ahead, dive in, and don't let performance anxiety make you end up looking like a "cioccolataio"—this is an expression that you will only understand if you're from Turin. In short, it refers to someone who appears pitiful or inadequate. It originates from an anecdote involving Duke Carlo Felice, who discovered that a chocolatier was parading around in a carriage identical to his. Naturally, he felt embarrassed and demanded a carriage with extra features to avoid being associated with the "cioccolataio."

Well, chocolatiers, carriages, and attention-seeking dukes aside, here's the thing: you've got to get your hands dirty and get hands-on experience. If you don't put yourself to the test, you'll lose that connection your memory has forged with the archetypes and the everyday situations that can be linked to each of the Arcana. Let me tell you, even I, in the beginning, was scared to assign a concept that seemed completely opposite to the person sitting across from me. But then it hit me, and it was an important realization: I'm not in an exam, and I'm not trying to play a guessing game to get the right meaning. I just need to open up my mind, like a dusty attic, and find that perfect archetype, and then present it to the person and explain it to them.

Even though I'm not a fan of cheesy or overly sentimental phrases, what I'm about to say is genuine and crucial: you need to open up, let your heart and gut speak, and allow the words to flow freely. But of course, never forget that you're dealing with an individual who has their own feelings and emotions, and it's essential to treat them with respect. On the flip side, always assert yourself and set your boundaries when it comes to conducting a session or pursuing Tarot reading as your lifelong career. There's a phrase that resonates with me, "do no harm, take no shit." Remember, you're not a punching bag for others to release their frustrations onto. Keep that in mind at all times!

All the very best
to you and your family

If you've found that your perspective on Tarot has shifted while reading this book, if you've seen yourself or someone familiar in its pages, if you'd gladly recommend it or even give it a second read, then I've achieved my mission in my own little way. Now, if none of what I've mentioned strikes a chord with you, well, you can't please everyone, can you? But if it does resonate with you, Bae, your support, reviews, and affection are truly cherished (and hey, if all goes well, maybe Lo Scarabeo will have me write another one 😌). So please, do share your thoughts and opinions, for they are immensely valuable to me. They help me gauge whether the work I've put into this book aids you in better comprehending this world, which often finds itself obscured by confusion, mysticism, and common misconceptions (but I'm sure you've already gathered that by now).

One evening, just before wrapping up everything on this book, I was having dinner with Sara, a former colleague and dear friend who has witnessed the birth and growth of my Tarot divination work on Instagram. As we raised our glasses in a toast, she uttered a profoundly impactful phrase that I quickly jotted down in my phone's notes, fearing its wisdom would slip away. And here it is, ingrained in my memory: "To all those who have ventured down the wrong path, believing it to be the right one." The beauty of this statement is its versatility across various domains of life. During the lockdown, I had the unique privilege of putting a halt to the wild and reckless race I was caught up in with my previous job. I am fully aware that this period wasn't favorable for most individuals, which is precisely why I use the term "privilege" with utmost significance. If I hadn't been caught off guard, without a job, without something to do, without anyone to talk to, I probably wouldn't have ended up on this path. This book wouldn't be in your hands, Bae wouldn't even exist, and the world of Tarot wouldn't have a fearless advocate striving every day to unleash its true potential. Maybe I would still be stuck in some suffocating place, believing it was the only right road to take because "that's just how it's always been, why bother questioning it?" Or perhaps I would have arrived here eventually, albeit at a slower pace—who knows? My genuine hope is that this book, the journey of learning to read Tarot (and read yourself), can unveil the wrong paths you might unknowingly be treading, reveal the existence of alternatives, and inspire you to give them serious consideration.

I want to publicly express my gratitude (oh no, here comes the part where my Cancer sign shows, and I become a crybaby!) to the people who have played a significant role in showing me the various paths available. First and foremost, my teacher Stella Noctis. She saw something special within me and helped me unearth it, just like dust gently swept from the hidden corners of a house (Stella, I hold your book, the first one on this transformative journey, as a cherished treasure). A big thank you also goes to my dearest friend, Chiara, who has been a constant presence during the most significant moments of my life. She has always pushed me to do great things (Chiara, I know this is a book and not a TV show, but I promise we'll get there too).

And to my old crappy job, if it weren't for you, I probably wouldn't have sought an alternative path in the study of Tarot. Matteo and Pippi, you guys are the best. I want you to know how much I love you and how grateful I am for you keeping an eye on me (okay, let's admit it, sometimes it felt like you were keeping me under surveillance) and helping me stay focused while writing. You've been my biggest supporters throughout these years, cheering me on and celebrating every milestone. And let's not forget about those times when I needed to disappear for a while to carve out a solid path in this direction—your understanding and support meant the world to me. And to my amazing astro-bitches of the heart, Alina and Roberto, you two have been my partners in crime, my comrades in the world of esotericism. Together, we've formed an unstoppable trio of "powerful women" (oh, Francesca Amara, the Wolf, you're definitely part of our crew!). Thank you for putting up with my daily rants and sharing in the wild adventures of this journey. Our bond is unbreakable. Some of the songs written on the Major Arcana cards actually came from the brilliant minds of my students who joined my courses throughout the years. Can you believe they trusted me enough to sign up? It still amazes me to this day, which is why I want to express my heartfelt gratitude to each and every one of them. You are not only present within the pages of this book but also constantly in my thoughts. And of course, a big thank you goes out to all the Baes who have chosen to have their cards read by me, regardless of whether you consider yourselves Ms. Betties or not. Your feedback has been absolutely invaluable over the years, guiding me in the right direction and helping me constantly improve my readings. I also want to give a special shoutout to the 1990s and 2000s, the decades that shaped me and influenced my pop culture references, sometimes venturing into the delightfully trashy territory. I love you all! And I hope that through my pages, you can relive those cherished moments too.

Lastly, but certainly not least, I would like to express my gratitude to the staff at Lo Scarabeo for giving me the opportunity to share my thoughts on a subject in which they are the absolute masters. Thank you for listening to my ideas, especially my graphic demands and delusions about how I wanted the book to be. You gave me free rein, and I hope not to disappoint your expectations. Otherwise, I'll proceed with a change of identity and move to Vanuatu. No problem at all.

Tarot cards, just like astrology (or any esoteric practices), shouldn't simply provide answers; their purpose is to ignite questions, foster debate, and challenge you to evaluate alternatives. Always question what you read, even what I've written in this book. The important thing is for you to develop a critical sense.

If you'd like, let's discuss it together.
You can find me on Instagram as @soloredie.

I dedicate this book to my sister Eleonora.
And to myself. Hey, toothy, you've done well!

The Author

Alice Mastroleo reads Tarot cards and teaches Cartomancy. Her passion for symbols, the esoteric, and revealing what is hidden has driven her to embark on a journey in these fields. Her love for pop culture has constantly led her to draw from this world to communicate the Arcana in a contemporary and fresh way. Born with the Sun in the Eighth House, she has always been fascinated by the mysteries of the human psyche and has dedicated the last ten years to deepening this interest. Her approach stimulates personal growth while also promoting fun and the pleasure of introspection without fear. A compulsive collector of perfumes, she has an almost obsessive veneration for Pippo Franco and Renato Pozzetto (Italian actors and TV presenters) and knows all the lines of former Italian Tarot reader Nascia Prandi by heart.